Building a School of One:

One School's Journey

Goshen High School's

efforts to increase rigor and support

every student

By Jim Kirkton and Phil Lederach

Edited by André Swartley

SCHOOL OF ONE

Practitioner Publishing
417 Constitution Avenue
Goshen, Indiana 46526
http://ghs.goshenschools.org/

This edition published by Practitioner Publishing by arrangement with
21st Century Printing Company, LLC, Goshen, Indiana.

ISBN 0-9777268-0-0

Dedicated to the entire staff
of Goshen High School
for their efforts to improve the opportunities
for the students in our community.
Special thanks go to the families as well,
for their support in this very demanding profession.

Acknowledgements

Thanks to the many people who have helped to write this book. All contributions no matter how large or small tell a significant piece of our story.

Jim Kirkton, Principal
Phil Lederach, Assistant Principal
Marceil Royer, Assistant Principal
Ted Mahnensmith, Assistant Principal
Larry Kissinger, Athletic Director
Bob Evans, Principal of Alternative School
Shelly Wilfong, Social Studies and Data Specialist
Barry Younghans, Central Office
Theresa Collins, Media Specialist
Carl Weaver, Chris Weaver, David Wilson, Ken Horst, Science
Jim Speicher, Judy Dalka, Anna Kridler, Cindy Swihart, Mathematics
Andre Swartley, Marilyn Graber, Scott Garvin, Sue Neeb, Richard Snyder, Jaime Shreiner, English
Dana Mehl, Jenny Clark, Social Studies
Barb Carbaugh and Jim Pickard, Physical Education
Jen Kalb, Special Education
Jim Graves and Chad Collins, German
Marcia Yost, Music
Cindy Cooper, Vince Brooks, Art
Ruth Comstock, Mary Jo Thomas, Guidance
Jane Brookmyer, FACS
Milt Thomas, Community
Jan Schrock, Secretary

http://ghs.goshenschools.org/

Table of Contents

To the Reader:

Anyone in field of education at this time, particularly public education, must show strong resolve in the face of constant criticism from political and public sources. America's public schools are not perfect, but we provide students with opportunities no other institutions can match. Our schools are open to all students, regardless of background, race, learning ability, or socio-economic class. Public schools are better equipped than any other institution to deal with the diversity that walks in the door each day.

Communities have poured their own resources into public schools and have a vested interest in their success. Teachers have devoted their careers to the education of the students in these communities. So what is the problem anyway?

Over the past few years, much research has gone into identifying the different generations currently living in America. These generations have been titled as follows, beginning with current school-age children and reaching to their great-grandparents: Millenials, Generation X'ers, Baby Boomers, and the Traditionalists. It is likely obvious to most educators that the Millenials are different from previous generations. That is not a value judgment; for good or ill, they are simply different.

Add into the mix that teachers working with these students come from four different generations and we begin to see the challenges facing public education. A system that was once set up as a factory to "mass produce" thousands of students with the same skills must now be tweaked to meet the needs of the 21st Century. And schools are not alone in this; the "typical" American workplace is changing rapidly as well. It is easy to understand the panic of the business community regarding education in America.

With the changing workplace, the system of education that was adequate in the past no longer provides the skills needed by the 21st century worker. That should suggest to fellow public school educators that we need to adjust how we do our business.

This book is about how Goshen High School is changing the way we do our business. Our focus is improving the rigor of our coursework and helping more students succeed within these increased expectations through creating a personalized environment. We have chosen to pursue this end through what we call a "School of One" initiative, which simply means that we think our students will excel in our system if each student feels himself/herself to be a significant part of our school. Students have always gotten lost in the shuffle, but this no longer is acceptable if students are to improve academic performance.

In this book, you will read some detail about this process from both the administration and the teaching staff. We do not work in a vacuum, nor do our students. We, like thousands of other schools, are simply doing our best to succeed in the real and changing world of public education. We have made some positive changes and we want to share those changes with the dual hopes of sparking discussion in the education community and continuing our own growth. Nothing could suit us better than sitting together and sharing ideas with educators from all types of schools all over the nation.

This book is a team effort just like the changes we have made. It is about successes and failures, but mostly it is about a bunch of dedicated teachers doing what they can to provide the best experiences possible for students. Nothing was done in a week, or a year for that matter; changes have occurred over a period of time. The key is that the changes are being applied to a learning model that governs all we do, and therein carries our message.

We are working at two things: improving student performance and enhancing teacher skill. This is all we will ever do. It is difficult to determine which comes first, student performance or teacher skill because they are so intertwined. We have included organization efforts that are general at best, along with departmental and individual teacher efforts. Sharing our stories has been a joy.

Jim Kirkton, Principal
Goshen High School
401 Lincolnway East
Goshen, IN 46526
574-533-8651

Chapter 1

One of the best times in my teaching career came from the daily discussions we had at lunch. Never did we allow our talk to be about the students. "Northern Exposure" and decoding the symbolism of that program began on Tuesday and lasted sometimes until Wednesday. Then it was on to sports, stories from our families, and even making fun of the administration. One topic we never broached, however, was that of how we taught. No teacher among us would dare talk about a successful teaching strategy because we did not want to seem pompous or self-centered. Anyone who has been in the classroom knows exactly what I am writing about. I taught next door to a wonderful English teacher for many years, but I never knew what she was doing. I knew the kids liked her classes, but I had no idea why. This is an unfortunate commentary on how schools have typically worked, at least until now. Now, any school that makes progress has teachers talking with each other about teaching. These professional learning communities provide hope for the future of public education.

Introduction

JIM KIRKTON, PRINCIPAL

This book is an attempt by the teachers and administrators of Goshen High School to summarize our journey as a school over the past four years. We are a school with a changing population and this is an account of steps we have taken to meet our constant challenges. Our hope in putting this book together is for educators to find ideas and support from our experiences and to encourage schools to initiate positive changes. We do not claim to have all the answers, but we can share what has worked and continues to work for us.

This effort got started when our assistant principal, Phil Lederach, made a statement during an administrative meeting with Marceil Royer and Ted Mahnensmith, that we need to write a practitioner's book to share our experiences. Finding articles or resources from practitioners involved in the nuts and bolts of the change process has become increasingly difficult. While we are sharing our experiences, we hope those who read this will also provide us additional insights for our journey.

An observation by one of our seasoned teachers was made at a department chair meeting that even with the vast potential of the Internet, there were fewer and fewer places to visit that would be of direct help to us. Our philosophy had been to visit anywhere that was doing a great job. Just where would that be? These Utopian schools were becoming harder and harder to find, and usually, when we got there, they were just like us, mere mortals. The conclusion was to initiate the process of creating a practitioners' resource book intended to begin conversations if not provide many answers.

For us, the talking about teaching has played out by forming professional learning communities even beyond the walls of our own school. We meet with, share with, and strategize with fellow teachers from all schools in our athletic conference. The sense is that there is so much good information to share that even this conference sharing can and should be expanded.

Now as a principal, I reflect on my own experiences, over 22 years in the classroom and the last 10 years in administration, for inspiration. I came into a position as principal of this school knowing that we need change, but with little in the way of a plan for that change. In fact, I had no plan. For the most part, I had more or less always operated alone. This book may be as much about the rewards of collaboration as it is about changing the climate of a school and improving academic performance of students.

The "Nation at Risk" report didn't settle well with me when it first burst onto the national scene about two decades ago. Having taught for 12 years in three different school corporations, I didn't want to hear that public schools were anywhere near the failing grade given in the controversial report. The talk in the teachers' lounge turned from "Northern Exposure" to discount this report as totally, completely, and overtly false.

"They just don't understand what we are going through. Kids just aren't motivated like the used to be." Being a little distrustful of political motivations for labeling public schools as failures, I set out to prove single-handedly that the report was incorrect. I assumed, wrongly I might add, that all other teachers would do the same. Besides token resentment, I saw little concern or added commitment from my colleagues.

Immediately my days grew longer. I had taught English at every level from seventh grade through seniors in my tenure. Throwing myself into everything I could do to make students feel like they were learning more, I added to my responsibilities—school newspaper, yearbook, North Central Association work, studying of the standardized tests, assisting with the school musical. It felt good that some students took the time when they left my classroom to say, "Thank you."

I lived for those moments. That is what all teachers live for: concrete validation of the caring and effort put into preparing and delivering lessons to help students gain mastery of my subject.

Unfortunately, when looking back, it was probably a wasted effort even though I was able to form some outstanding relationships with all types of students. Why was this a wasted effort? Twenty years later, the reports say nothing has changed in public schools. In fact, there are pundits out there claiming that it may even be worse. All my work and effort seem to have done nothing to keep public schools off the negative radar of the state and national level politicians. Whenever they want to make some points with the public, they look at schools and utter some disturbingly familiar words like, "You can't fix it by throwing money at it."

In my unscientific experiment to single-handedly deflect state and national criticism, I worked myself into a frenzied state and accomplished nothing other than modest appreciation from a few of my students.

Twenty years later I am beginning to understand why all of my efforts didn't stop the attacks. The problem was that I was trying to do it by myself. In fact, all of the 40 plus teachers in my building were working by themselves. We never talked to each other. We never planned together outside the traditional book adoption years or North Central evaluation years. We behaved like independent contractors; we did our own thing.

As we spiral to the 21st century, I have gained a different perspective on the business of doing public school. It is not that the job has gotten easier. I have moved three times since "Nation at Risk" was published. In each case the job got harder. Currently, I am a high school principal in an urban high school in Goshen, Indiana. Our school has the largest English as a New Language (ENL) population in our state. Our district population includes over 21 percent ENL students and our high school has over a 40 percent poverty rate. Corporation wide, more than one third of our students are minority students. In our cafeteria we have posted over 30 flags representing the various birth countries of our students.

When I became principal of this school four years ago, I had no idea of what to do about our nemesis, the "Nation at Risk" report. Staring us in the face were new accountability measures from the state of Indiana called Public Law 221. This law requires community and parent based committees to declare a mission, vision, and plan for improving school performance, primarily on the state graduation qualifying exam. There are high-stakes consequences built into this program if schools do not make acceptable progress.

No Child Left Behind (NCLB) was not yet conceived. No one had devised the current rapidly changing graduation requirements. Even without these hurdles, I had no idea how to take what has proven to be a fairly simple first step. However, I did understand that merely asking or expecting teachers to work longer hours would not bring about any long-range cures.

Serving as an assistant principal in the late 1990's, I was called to a meeting about graduation rate. The superintendent and I were to meet with two representatives from the state department to discuss why our graduation rates were so low. The previous two years we had reported a graduation rates of 71 and 78 percent. Our accreditation was on the line. In the course of our conversation I promised the State Department representatives that I would do whatever it took to correct this situation. This sounded amazingly similar to my failure as a teacher to fix the entire system by myself.

The graduation rates had only peaked a year or two but definitely needed attention. We were able to make some improvements particularly through expansion of alternative school opportunities beginning in 1998-1999.

1987-88	64.10%
1988-89	64.50%
1989-90	78.40%
1990-91	83.00%
1991-92	70.70%
1992-93	69.90%
1993-94	78.10%
1994-95	73.60%
1995-96	75.70%
1996-97	76.50%
1997-98	71.40%
1998-99	78.50%
1999-00	84.40%
2000-01	91.60%
2001-02	89.80%

I pleaded with these state department officials to give me some ideas. I promised to camp at the schools in our state that faced similar demographic issues we faced in Goshen and copy their programs to turn around our fortunes. Surely some similar school had found success. The State Department's response was less than encouraging. Their only answer was that the statistics of schools would be posted on the state website.

Later, when I checked the website and plugged in the parameters, I realized I had misinterpreted their silence; the real reason they did not answer was that they *had* no answer. There were no examples in our entire state of schools with similar demographics that had succeeded in registering the levels of excellence required by the state.

Most educators had heard, and it was widely accepted by educators, that there is no need to take standardized tests. Demographers can predict the results of the test with amazing accuracy based on the population of the school. Those of us teaching in poverty or minority schools are doomed to the public scrutiny and the attacks from the skeptics simply because of types of students we teach. Again there was nothing I could do about it, no matter how hard I tried.

Somehow the inspectors allowed us to slide by without removing our state accreditation. We had started an alternative program and there was hope on the horizon. Little did we know that within a couple of years, we would be approaching the magical 90 percent level with the alternative program and several other initiatives, so their confidence was justified.

But graduation rate was only the beginning and perhaps the easiest of the hurdles we had to face. Looming on the horizon were several years of declining test scores. Scores were declining in almost direct correlation with the increases in second language and minority enrollment. The new accountability law would highlight any of our weaknesses when we posted our data in the newspaper.

In the following graph, Core 40 and Academic Honors diplomas are desirable degrees for those wishing to go to some type of post-secondary schooling. Poverty students face challenges as compared to paid lunch students.

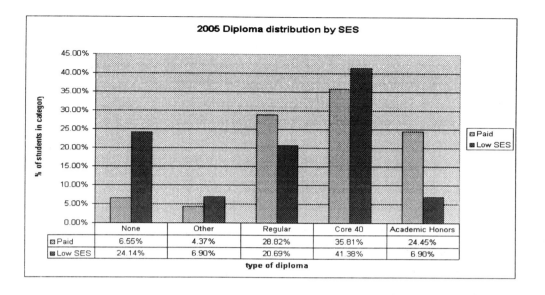

type of diploma	None	Other	Regular	Core 40	Academic Honors
Paid	6.55%	4.37%	28.82%	35.81%	24.45%
Low SES	24.14%	6.90%	20.69%	41.38%	6.90%

But we could not do our business hidden under a rock, and good news once in a while does not hold much water in the public's view. We had to do something that would build positive results over a period of years. The search was on.

I began by making promises to the faculty. First of all, they were suffering from the same competitive frustration I had been through. They were working harder every year with little success. Teachers in schools with different student demographics were taking credit for being good teachers because of their reported results while we continued to be looked at in a negative sense because of the falling scores. There is no way to explain to someone outside the corporation that there was a legitimate reason for this; there is no excuse for an excuse, so our staff just shouldered the criticism. But they did not like it. They wanted to win at this game. They wanted their students to win at this game. There was too much at risk to allow the state's concept of accountability to categorize us in bold letters.

Two promises stick out the most in my memory. The first was that we would find a way to stop the bleeding. We would travel nation-wide if necessary to get help, to learn about and bring back new learning models. The second promise was that we would not work more hours than we already do. This brought about more than a few snickers. Conventional wisdom dictated that working harder is the only option we had for success. Political pundits proffer often that teacher effort or lack thereof is what ails the educational system.

When I made those promises, I had no idea whether I could keep them or not, but I would try; they were good places to start. In the meantime we still had the same job to do and everyone soon became busy with the everyday tasks of being a teacher.

What follows are practitioners' attempts to use the best of the most highly accepted research in a school improvement. Maybe those reading this book will discover some patterns that have worked or will work, avoid some of the pitfalls we encountered, take our ideas to further successes, or simply gain the courage to begin their own journeys.

The graph below shows the changing demographics of our school corporation. With our changing populations, we were faced with new challenges. Most of our new students are second language learners coming mostly from Latino countries but also coming from all continents all over the world.

Percent of population from 1996-97 through 2003-04

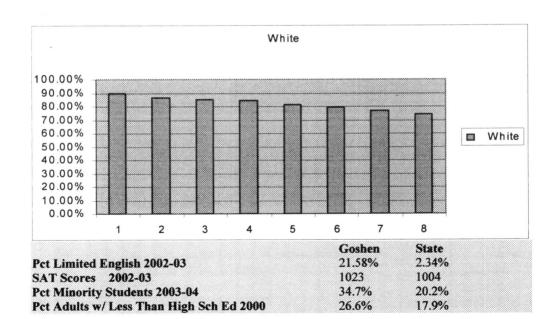

	Goshen	State
Pct Limited English 2002-03	21.58%	2.34%
SAT Scores 2002-03	1023	1004
Pct Minority Students 2003-04	34.7%	20.2%
Pct Adults w/ Less Than High Sch Ed 2000	26.6%	17.9%

Chapter 2

In improving our school we needed to have something concrete at the center of our efforts. We found a learning model that we felt could define our intentions and would definitely improve student performance. The learning model became just the beginning, but it gives us a central focus to rally around. There is nothing unusual or exceptional about this model. Rather it is a simple formula to guide a very complex process. Logic is what we needed.

The Learning Model

JIM KIRKTON, PRINCIPAL

Where are the schools that have changing populations, particularly in the areas of increased poverty students, Limited English Proficient (LEP) students, and minority students? What have schools done to be successful with closing the gaps in learning among the disaggregated populations? How did they do it?

Following our meeting with the State Department about needing to improve our program, we asked them for help. Their answer was not what we wanted to hear because they really did not know of any schools that seemed to be showing improvement through the changing of demographics.

Almost all schools champion their teaching staffs because they are caring individuals, they are leaders in their community, and they want what is best for students. At the beginning of the process, our teaching staff embodied all of these characteristics. There was a definite sense that we were victims of circumstances beyond our control. We needed a new vision to be our guiding principle through the good and bad times we knew we still had to face, and likely more of the latter. The first glimmer came in a session at the North Central Association convention in Chicago in the spring of 2002. Finally there was research stating that in the United States there were six school corporations with higher minority, poverty, and LEP enrollments beginning to make some type of headway in performance. Some of the data was preliminary, but there were signs that schools dealing with changing demographics could make adjustments and improve anyway.

As we examined these schools, some common themes came to light. These school corporations had adopted the stance that *all students can learn.* Given that premise, these schools and teachers needed to change how they approached instruction.

Goshen High School, being a typical secondary school, is prime evidence that teachers love the subjects they teach; after all, most teachers were at one time successful students in the educational system. In addition, they have gained a love for their subject area concentrations. Because of this, we really are about "what we teach."

Teachers in improving schools changed their classroom focus away from subject material to monitoring what students actually learned. That single concept struck a chord with us because it makes so much sense. But it also creates huge problems. In order to change focus to monitoring and guaranteeing what students are learning, we would have to turn the business of doing school in a totally different direction.

It might not be hard to get one teacher to understand how this learning model would work. It might not be hard to get even 10 teachers to understand this new approach. But, we have well over 80 teachers. Moving this large staff from understanding to practice would be a challenge that we wanted to work on for the next year, but realistically we knew that this would be an ongoing focus for the next several years. Not only that, the components of working this learning model could take years to refine. NCLB would not give us this kind of time. NCLB demands quantitative yearly improvement.

We have told our staff that all improving schools are doing the same thing. This was a big statement founded on the fact that relatively few schools were actually improving. Some stayed the same or within a range, but not many had actually shown a significant statistical growth in student performance over any length of time. Couple that with the fact that schools are run by people who have been successful in the current system and we began to understand why changing to a new learning model would be a daunting task.

Now the major question is, "What is a learning model?"

Our staff asked this question over and over. When we were done explaining the components, we rarely heard complaints or disagreements that following this new learning model would improve student performance. The tough questions boiled down to *how?* What about time? What about standards? What responsibility does the student have? Why do I have to work with others? Does this mean I have been doing it wrong all of these years? Each question is significant and each question had to be answered.

Since all of the instructional models used in these improving schools were alike, and since most of the research done in education supported similar processes, why were there eight-step models, three-step models, and five-step models? We needed a plan and we had to be able to communicate it to our staff.

For the entire year, the administrators studied DuFour's and Eaker's book *Professional Learning Communities That Work*. Because we liked the administrative approach and banked on their successes, we enrolled in a HOPE Conference (Hope Foundation) in Columbus, Ohio, to hear Rick DuFour talk about school improvement. What we got was a lot more than just an educational conference. DuFour put legs on the talk about measuring learning instead of teaching. It was so sensible that I became very excited.

DuFour talked about a three-step model, paraphrased below:

1. **Decide what you are going to teach.**
2. **Assess it.**
3. **Do something about it.**

We were attracted to the brevity and simplicity of his message. The overall implications of those three steps are enormous and have been center stage in all we have done since that time. In American education, we hardly ever get to DuFour's second step, and if we do get there we often assess either something different from or something more than we taught. Because of time constraints and our acceptance of the Bell Curve, we *never* get to step three. Convincing teachers to act on their assessments seemed at first to be a major hurdle. The Bell Curve teaches us that a certain percentage of the students are not going to get it or don't deserve to get it because of the widely accepted range of individual intelligence suggested by the curve. Certainly a Bell Curve does not follow the literal meaning of No Child Left Behind. As educators, we believe that intelligence impacts learning, but given enough time, all students can learn.

The first step, deciding what to teach, seemed like a natural step for teachers, yet it required much preparation and time for the staff to realize what it meant. We called upon

strong leaders throughout the staff to direct their colleagues in organizing curriculum based on the standards.

Our teachers' initial responses to the learning model were both positive and guarded. Two groups of twenty teachers were invited to full-day workshops at the Chamber of Commerce to look at how our vision would evolve into a school-wide plan. Developing the vision had been a challenging task, but the staff responded that our mission and vision really were sound approaches for our students.

The mission statement, "Ensuring all students acquire knowledge and apply skills—enhancing tomorrow's opportunities," seemed to be well understood. The vision statement built what we wanted our school to look like. Both statements were built through staff and community input. Most importantly, though, our staff agreed with them. These statements became the test for our school improvement plan required by the State of Indiana.

GHS After Hours

Some students need extra time in order to be successful, and GHS After Hours provides just that. The idea for After Hours originated from and is funded by our Smaller Learning Community grant. This program keeps the library open 10 extra hours after school per week and is staffed by one media resource person and one teacher. For students needing transportation home, we provide a late bus at 5:30 p.m. The program serves around 30 students nightly with that number being closer to 40-50 during the crunch times before tests or project due dates. Students use this time to finish projects for many classes across the curriculum—the primary areas including major projects include science, social studies, health, ENL, and English. Sometimes teachers also leave make-up assignments or tests to be completed by their students during this time.

Other students use the After Hours time because they need the technology we have to offer at GHS. Many of our kids don't have computers readily available outside of school, and After Hours provides the extra time to finish projects and papers they need outside of the time provided in class and SRT. Other students may have a computer at home, but they don't have the programs we have, such as Publisher or PowerPoint. Sometimes students also meet with their mentors during this extension of the school day. Still others work on PLATO, a self-paced and individualized software program aligned to Indiana standards.

By providing more time for students to finish assignments, After Hours plays an important role in helping many kids to be successful. Students also undoubtedly benefit from the individual help provided by both the media resource person and the teacher. The staff people find themselves busy helping with homework assignments, finding research materials, and providing technical assistance. They also spend quite a bit of time helping ENL students with language issues associated with reading assignments and research materials.

After completing the first year of this program, we'll make a few adjustments for next year. During the past year, we were open until 6 p.m. on Monday, Wednesday, and Thursday and 8 p.m. on Tuesday. The kids didn't really make use of the time after 6 p.m. on Tuesdays like we had thought they might, so we'll stay open only until 6 p.m. Monday through Thursday next year. We close at 4 p.m. on Friday; and in the beginning, we wondered if we should stay open until 6 p.m. on Friday nights too; however, after tracking the usage throughout the year, the numbers on Friday do not really warrant that.

Staffing has been a struggle; these are difficult hours to find someone to work. We also feel like it is important not to rotate these hours between several staff members because the students count on seeing certain staff members here after school. I think these relationships are something else that can be important in helping our students to be successful—this also contributes to developing the School of One. Throughout the past semester, it became obvious that many students were looking for a place to work in which they felt comfortable and safe and we've provided just that by including our After Hours Program.
-THERESA COLLINS, Media Specialist

What the school improvement plan did not include was an organized process for actually showing the desired gains. The learning model would put wings to our plan and bring the improvement into all classrooms.

After our day at the Chamber, different groups around our school began the first process of instilling the learning model into daily classroom routine. We had started the year by doing book studies with randomly assigned groups. In all, we had 14 groups who were given the latitude to read and study books of their choosing. The only requirement was that the books were to be about best practice in education or student learning.

"Best practice" is an elusive term because it can cover so many topics. Groups studied books on: children in poverty, writing throughout the curriculum, brain-based learning concepts, the psychology of learning, and reading in the content areas. Minutes from each meeting were submitted to the principals, who compiled them in a monthly staff newspaper called Study to Practice (STP) Minutes. Our assistant principal, Phil Lederach, even copied the STP oil logo for use on the newsletter banner.

The biggest change STP meetings brought about was a collegial feeling among staff members in different departments. They were talking with other teachers about their profession and enjoying it. Teachers who had dwelt in closed-door classrooms for years began sharing their experiences with others. Exchanging stories of both success and failure with students also created new trust among teachers.

However, the study groups, while enjoyable, soon had to be specialized. Now teachers would be studying within their own departments, something that had been reserved for ordering paperclips and the selection of books in adoption years. That meant that sometime during the remainder of that year, each teacher would meet with the other teachers who taught the similar courses to plan units and assessments for those units, and do something about them.

Our new practices, as one might expect, very quickly generated epiphanies and changes in the way we did our business:

- **Not everyone agreed on what is essential learning for a course—the state standards are usually more extensive than can comfortably fit in a semester, and teachers had to prioritize.**
- **They agreed on the essential learning and shared possible teaching strategies if given time.**
- **The workload in preparing the unit was shared (delivering on the promise we would not require more time of them).**
- **Teachers would spend time instructing the students only on what they planned to assess.**
- **Teachers developed plans to enact if students were unsuccessful on assessments.**

Some groups, which we labeled, "course-alike," functioned well, and others struggled because of clashing personalities. However, like all professions, teaching demands a certain degree of maturity—two professionals need not necessarily like one another to complete a task successfully.

The groups met before school for the most part, but soon asked for days of professional leave. This was a welcome request because it meant that teachers were ready to spend the time to plan and the planning would be thorough. It also allowed us to prove that we as administrators hoped to improve student performance without teachers spending more time outside their jobs. These short morning meetings eventually reduced individual planning time, and the professional leave times would save evening and weekend hours that teachers typically give to their preparations. The teachers reported to us that they were getting more than just a well-planned unit. They began to feel the benefits of working together toward a common goal.

Course-alike groups were asked to report their progress, and during the rest of that year all teachers made some type of effort to plan their units. The most eager groups were courses like English and math, which faced state and national accountability.

Biology pitched in quickly as well, as we had drastically increased the number of freshmen taking that course. Two years prior, fewer than 50 percent of the freshmen came into Goshen High School on a college bound track meaning that they took a course called Science Fundamentals. This particular year, 85 percent of the students were enrolled in Biology I. This was a good thing, but took tremendous coordination. Course-alike meetings helped the six biology teachers plan lessons for students with a wider range of abilities. Now, all freshmen will be enrolled in biology as the entry-level high school course.

Most school corporations write curriculum in book adoption years, and then individual teachers mold the new curriculum to their own styles. The new groups we formed helped to guarantee the consistency of classroom curriculum for all students, regardless of who taught a given course. This is still an ongoing process two years later, but continues to be an exciting time for teachers who dearly love their subjects and love teaching them to their students.

The beauty of the learning model is that all parts of it can be a focus at any time. Generally speaking, we do not think our curriculum will ever be perfect; therefore it will be under constant scrutiny by our teaching staff as they review the curriculum in their course meetings. This means a textbook will never dictate curriculum. Rather, professional teachers have ultimate control over how and when they teach the content and skills mandated by the state.

Assessing student learning in the form of a grade has been a standard practice for teachers probably since the beginning of schools. In this learning model, though, assessment is not to establish a letter grade, but to measure actual student learning. This is a big change.

The second step of the learning model, assessment, actually began almost simultaneously with the discussion of what was essential in our courses. Traditionally, assessing for grades followed the Bell Curve's prescription of separating students by performance. But, in using the learning model, we were concerned only with students learning what we describe as essential. The power of this concept is considerable.

We tracked students who had failing marks in at least one class at the end of the first grading period. This created a little stir among the staff for a number of reasons. There were questions about how much scrutiny administration was going to have in the grading process. One major concern was that teachers would lower their standards to pass more students.

Undoubtedly, many other concerns were never even voiced. The real reason for tracking student failures was to try to get a handle on the learning that was taking place in our school. We also knew that failures are not a perfect measure, but tracking failures gave us a starting point for looking at our students.

Assuming that grades actually reflect learning, assessment should give us some idea of student learning. We found that the majority of students failed because they either did not complete their required coursework or else were absent too often—usually these were related. Suddenly we realized a failing grade may say nothing at all about a student's learning or a teacher's teaching. This concept of defining what a failing grade means is the dilemma, and this is the dilemma of a school improvement effort.

We needed to reshape our assessments to tell us what the students know while functioning and participating in our guaranteed curriculum. This brought about the development of common assessments for comparison at various points within courses. The first thought was to create unit tests. The trouble with this is that although teachers could see what students had or had not learned, it was too late for students to do anything about it.

Goshen High School Dollars for Scholars (GHSDFS) began in 1991. The format is simple—local funds are raised and distributed annually to graduating seniors at Goshen High School. GHSDFS has a governing board, a fundraising committee, and a scholarship selection committee. It is affiliated with the Citizen's Scholarship Foundation of America.

This affiliation enables most students that receive a scholarship from GHSDFS to apply for a matching grant from the school he or she plans to attend. Colleges receive grants when they partner with the Citizen's Scholarship Foundation of America and are required to pass a portion of these funds on to students with Dollars for Scholars awards.

The GHS Guidance Department advertises the GHS DFS Scholarships to the students by including a written narrative about each scholarship in the Common Application Form, distributing and explaining these Common Application Forms to all GHS Seniors and finally "sorting out" students who have received extensive scholarships so that the GHS DFS Scholarship Selection Committee can spread out the scholarships to more students. We avoid situations where local scholarship dollars replace financial aid offered from the college and in this way, the counselors help support our goal to encourage as many graduating seniors as possible to continue his or her education at the post high school level. Statistics show that students, who have success in their first year of post high school education, have greater aid possibilities for further education.

For the past few years, GHSDFS has awarded about seventy students with scholarships that total $100,000 annually. The source of these annual funds comes actually from three sources:

1. Interest from funds invested by the Elkhart County Community Foundation. The base funds originate from Goshenites' wills and estates.
2. Annual contributions from anyone in Goshen to the general fund.

3. Annual contributions of $1,000 or more from individuals, clubs or groups, businesses, etc. for memorial scholarships.
    GHSDFS is always proud to announce that virtually all locally collected dollars go to scholarships for GHS graduating seniors. GHS Dollars for Scholars is a true non-profit organization.
    -MILT THOMAS, President

Teachers can always make adjustments for the next year, but students have no such luxury. To make unit common assessments effective, course-alike groups considered modifying standard procedures. Perhaps students could take a test multiple times. If we accepted that the purpose of an assessment was to measure true learning and prepare students for the next layers of a course—not to trick or punish them—there was undeniable logic to multiple testing opportunities.

No matter what, simply slapping a grade on a student's test and shoving him or her down the assembly line to perform the same way on the next test and the next was no longer acceptable. As we conquer each unit, some students will learn all of what we expect, but others will miss out on critical understandings, and this effect compounds with each successive unit and year. Master's-level students within the GHS faculty have brought us articles showing that often a few extra hours of help would have actually recovered a student who seems so far behind. **The last step was to "do something" about the results of an assessment. Some models referred to this as either** *tutorial* **or** *remediation*. **The toughest question was what to do with the students who needed no remediation while we worked with the ones who did. There was a word for this too:** *enrichment*. **On paper, it sounds simple—the successful students could learn extra skills or content about the previous unit for their own academic edification. In practice, enrichment looms as another challenge in transforming ourselves from a teaching school to a learning school.**

The science department caught the vision first and made plans to "do something about it." With the increased numbers of students enrolled in biology, there were multiple sections of biology in any one period. Their idea was to use every Monday as a tutorial/enrichment day. A common assessment would show them which students needed enrichment or tutorial and they would be divided fairly among the teachers every Monday. This was initially a lot of work, but showed immediate improvement.

Enrichment was a real challenge. High school teachers are not used to the privilege of taking students deeper into their subjects, so they devised entirely new plans. Tutorial activities were often based on brain research, but certainly simple reviews made a difference. This held true for LEP students in particular.

Okay, so students were doing better in a more difficult unit. This was exciting, but administratively we were concerned; this learning model was not less work for the teachers. In fact, it was a lot more work. It would work until the initial rush of success wore off, but we had to establish a successful practice for the long haul. We formed committees to find more ways to provide students with extra time. Their parameters were to find time within the school day because that is the only time we can truly be accountable for students.

In the typical American school, we have grown to accept the concept that education revolves around time. If time is the constant in the system, then learning will be the variable. When we adjusted the time in this way, or in any of the ways listed in other parts of the book, learning increased. So varying time is a more acceptable concept than varying the learning.

Summary

Change is not a straight line. Adopting a model to serve as the litmus for any school improvement activities provided us with the foundation for all that was to come. Certainly, the learning model of 1) deciding what to teach according to standards, 2) assessing for learning, and 3) doing something about it *is a logical first step and got us going, but it is only the centerpiece of our journey. There is much more to do as we strive to create a school climate in which each student feels welcomed and valued. Our two pronged journey of improving student academic performance and refining teaching skills was and is a crooked road filled with ruts and obstacles.*

Chapter 3

Improving the art and skill of teaching historically has been dictated by the initiative of individual teachers, partly because hit-and-miss directives from administration have plagued staff development. We have learned that coming up with ideas is easy enough, but turning an idea into useful practice and measuring its successes or failures are the difficult tasks. Administrators frequently just present an idea and, believing the work to be finished, move on to the next issue without getting anything done. When staff development comes from teachers working with each other, the learning has a much better chance to improve practice. Staff development should drive change in the classroom, but in reality change is nothing more than teachers working with each other to provide improved learning experiences for students.

Staff Development

JIM KIRKTON, PRINCIPAL

Educational research is a constant process throughout the academic community. It has produced significant information and resultant programming for schools. In my experience over the last two decades, school years typically begin with outstanding educators/orators sharing their stories in engaging and humorous ways. Following the keynote speech, the staff attend breakout sessions led by peers or other speakers. We learn about how great it is to be teachers, how teachers serve as mentors saving students from demise, and how to manage our classrooms effectively. Much inspiration comes from the orators' stories of being terrible students and "beating the odds" to become the college professors or educational consultants they are. Usually, we have opportunity to purchase their books *for only $29.95!*

After this, teachers return to their rooms and to reality. Soon there will be students, papers, grades, and routine. Lost, often before the next day, is the connection between the speaker and the classroom. Sure, we hear the statement, "That's the best in-service we have ever had" as departing educators recount their own stories not unlike those that the orator used to trump his or her point.

Moving from passively absorbing staff development as a teacher to being an administrator responsible for staff development caused me to re-examine its usefulness. The dollars used to bring in an expert for a day or two could fund much more valuable training.

School improvement efforts almost unanimously make staff development a central focus, but what should staff development look like? My experiences, as well as those of my administrative colleagues, on the receiving end staff development have steered us away from the solitary and short-lived blazes of glory from motivational speakers toward developing our staff thoughtfully over a longer period of time.

If staff development were defined as what teachers learn, incorporating the learning model into the planning would make excellent sense. As administrators we would 1) define essential learning for teachers, 2) assess that learning, and 3) do something with the information we gained from the assessment—follow the very process we expect the teachers to adopt for their own classrooms.

Our discussions regarding teachers' essential learning have included the following topics and changes: Public Law 221 (Indiana's school improvement plan), improving our attitude toward our job, defining common curriculum, establishing student resource time, using Bloom's Taxonomy to increase expectation and performance, teaching reading in high school, writing in subject areas, and studying effective teaching strategies. If we as administrators were to follow the learning model with staff development, we would somehow assess the staff's learning and use this information to design future staff development sessions.

While this, in theory, is how we should create staff development, implementing this protocol has come more slowly. First we had to accept that staff development and classroom instruction are similar, if not totally alike. Planning for staff development would have to be more thorough than ever if we wanted to assess the results. The three following steps are the most basic and important ones we followed. The steps might come in different sequences depending on a school's makeup, but they are all critical for a staff development plan to become the fabric of growth for a school.

Step One: Staff becomes a learning community

When I first moved into the role as chief administrator, I took little time to study to process of improving a school academically. In addition to this, the entire staff was really not on target for what was needed for school improvement. For years we administrators planned and discussed, but usually we went with our instincts; when in doubt, trust your instincts. Once the instincts became the plan we moved ahead, never to return. Eventually we lost sight of our planned intention in a myriad of new ideas, eventually coming back to where we started, almost without realizing it. A standing joke among educators is that if you don't get on board the first time, just wait a while and it will return later. Conversely, if you don't like a suggested change, just be patient—it will soon go away.

Listing all of the ideas for educational change in the last twenty years would be a book in itself, but surely no one can forget open classrooms or outcome based learning. Long discussions also occurred on block schedules and new math. Educators sitting around a room recalling old programs can literally work themselves into a state of hysteria by just bringing up the names.

Those who resisted the changes were right—those changes went away. They went away because the ideas were not based on the learning model process. These programs were not necessarily based on solid research, they were not assessed for implementation and effect, and there were no corrective measures taken if there were shortcomings.

The underpinnings

None of these processes will work if you cannot get them started. If as an administrator, I could not intelligently talk about "best practice" with my staff, where could I start? The year before we began, we studied DuFour's book on professional learning communities, but since This book was oriented towards administrators, it had little relevance for a teacher in the classroom.

Through our administrative meetings, we identified areas of concern for teachers. From this we composed an entire list of topics that we were careful to say were only suggestions:

Topics
I Read It But I Don't Get It
Defeating non-performance
Discipline with Dignity
EASIER reading program volunteers
Classroom Management
Ruby Payne
Raccoon Circles
Study to Practice

| Increasing Success of ENL |
| Implementing Best Practice in Classrooms |
| Motivating Students |
| ???? Your choice |

On the first day of school, the entire staff was divided into random groups of seven or eight teachers, according to preparation period. Our challenge to the staff was to meet once every month and discuss a chapter of their chosen book. Since they each had common preps, they could use 30 or 40 minutes of their 90-minute prep period. As it turned out, the groups mostly chose to meet in the hours before school to preserve preparation time. Groups selected topics, ordered appropriate books, and met to discuss their findings.

It was not long before positive comments came from all areas of the building. Teachers do not usually talk about education, often because they are afraid of offending colleagues or being offended them. The books made discussion natural. The book discussions also integrated our typically isolated secondary staff into multi-disciplinary groups. Administratively, we met with a selected leader from each group on Friday mornings to check on their progress and troubleshoot any problems.

For the first three months, prior to the chopped up holiday season, all flowed very well. The professional library now housed 100 new books and teachers were reading them. We laughed at how foolish it is to be in the education business and not be more informed of the latest developments.

One caveat we agreed upon was to steer clear of program reading. All books were about the business of education, not some prescribed program. The purpose was to think about our profession and talk with our peers. In retrospect, the groups were too loosely organized to survive long, and because of later initiatives, this part of staff development soon passed. But it was not a flash in the pan. We made a discovery that we declared was purposeful, but was probably blind luck: *teachers like to talk with each other about teaching.* When given this opportunity, they will make new friendships and share a wide variety of experiences.

Step Two: Researching and understanding the learning model

A common fear that teachers have when something "new" comes down the pike is that this concept will negate every teaching method they have ever used, including successful ones. The learning model certainly emphasizes a different aspect to teaching by redefining assessment, but does not remove the teacher from the formula.

We had already created a successful environment for discussion. Some of the reading about best practice even reinforced the necessity of providing an outstanding curriculum based on the standards for each course. Teachers who typically insist on creating and delivering the curriculum by themselves registered no real loss. The learning model gets credence from teachers because it offers a structured forum for teachers to make curricular decisions and ultimately share some of the workload.

Administration—Newly Arrived

I came to Goshen High School as an administrator after teaching for five years in a rural community just 15 miles away from Goshen. Although I had lived in Goshen for 4 years, I had no concept of the diversity in our town until I stepped into GHS.

What attracted me to GHS was the interview process itself. The principal talked about the culture of his building as being a "learning community," and that the focus of the school had shifted from teaching to learning, and that given enough time and support all students could learn.

It was easy to see that these educational leaders really modeled what they believed as they helped teach me how to deal with discipline as a level of intervention and time for learning and interaction with the students. Strategies that I had used with students in the past needed to be revised as I worked with a student body of nearly 40 percent poverty and 30 percent new language learners. When I called parents, I often dealt with parents who did not value education or accused me of being racist. I personally worked on several skills: patience; understanding issues from a poverty or minority perspective; and above all, listening to and respecting the input of each student and parent that came in my door. I often worked with translators, asked a lot of questions, and tried to come up with creative ways to look past the symptoms of behavior and deal with root issues.

I developed a handout for students and parents that illustrated the school's levels of offense so parents and/or students did not feel like I was targeting them personally with a given disciplinary action. When students came into my office (over 1800 referrals the first year) I looked up their grades and attendance and begin the intervention with that information. I worked with the school nurse and guidance to develop non-smoking clinics and anger management "opportunities" for students. Of course, there were still suspensions and expulsions, but our first priority was and is to keep students in school and out of the principal's office.

-MARCEIL ROYER

We have a staff of nearly 90 teachers. As in any large gathering, groups tend to be dominated by a few who are willing to speak up. These more vocal staff members can sidetrack a discussion on short notice. But school improvement also cannot be a lecture. Even the best of intentioned and most planned presentations do little to develop staff ownership and actual understanding of difficult concepts.

What teachers need is time to process the information. What teachers need is small groups to process new ideas from administrators. An early release day may not be the forum because of this necessary processing time. Taking these into consideration, our administrative team—principals, head of guidance, athletic director—brainstormed how to best approach the beginning of long term staff development based on the learning model. Even in our inexperience, we all recognized that the next step was critical and would take time; DuFour took 17 years! We kept reminding ourselves of this, but our hearts said to go for it.

Finally we decided to use the Goshen Chamber of Commerce meeting room and spend two full days training two groups of about twenty teachers each. These groups would give us critical mass in implementing the staff development for the learning model. These teachers were already leaders and many were willing to walk into new challenges in teaching and school organization.

The Curriculum Council met first. This group consisted of various department heads, counselors, and administrators. Because several of the department chairs were shared positions, we actually had two representatives from English, math, and social studies, bringing additional key players into our initial meeting. We began by passing on research showing that schools with challenging demographics and improving performance all functioned with a learning model similar to ours.

To highlight the point, our vocational coordinator related his experience as an auto mechanics teacher. To fit in all mandated curriculum, he first went to local garages to determine what were the absolute essentials for his students. In the end, he came up with 17 different skills he wanted his students to master during his class, represented in his classroom by a chart. The students knew his expectations and could organize themselves to complete the course requirements. His methods also did not preclude input from another teacher, should others teach the same class in the future.

This scenario was logical and organized. The standards assisted the students in accomplishing the goals. The organization of the course was built around student learning and constant assessment. The assessments were such that if a student did not master the concept, additional instruction and time could be devoted to learning the concept.

The prevailing attitude in education at that time identified teachers as deliverers of information. If students were willing and able to absorb this information, they learned. If not, the common staff answer would be, "I told them, but they just didn't get it," and teachers would move on anyway. Eventually certain students would get so far behind that they would either give up totally or move themselves into a more protected area (an easier class) where they could be successful.

Outside critics of education do not understand the learning model. They say better teaching will improve learning, and to a degree they are right. But the real remedy begins with how we organize our instruction into chunks that students can understand based on what the standards mandate. Standards set much of the curriculum, but teachers must design the order and pacing for learning to happen. The learning model assists in this process and takes it well beyond the "I told them" approach.

We then looked outside the typical classroom for inspiration. Our choir has been a state champion. To be a state champion in anything is a great accomplishment. Our school has won state championships in football and individual state championships in wrestling and track. Others have competed successfully at the state level in individual and team sports. Band and orchestra have been to the state finals many times. What could we learn from those folks? How did they get there?

The Choral Program

The Goshen High School Choral Program consists of four concert choirs, two of which select members by audition only. We also have an excellent show-choir, the Crimsonaires, which performs approximately 40 times per year. In order for a student to be eligible for the show choir, the student needs to be in a concert choir as well. We have found that this is the only way to stress involvement in what we see as the lifeline of our organization: the concert choir. The show choir does not do the competition circuit. We are philosophically opposed to too much competition. However, we are not opposed to meaningful competition as it fits our educational journey.

The Goshen High School Advanced Crimson Choir has been ranked in the State of Indiana among the top ten choirs for more than a decade. Our advanced choral groups have participated in festivals in New York City, Washington, D.C., Toronto, and Montreal, receiving numerous championship honors. In the past 18 years no choral organization at GHS has received less than a superior rating at choir contests in Indiana or elsewhere.

All of this has been achieved and maintained even as the demographics in the city of Goshen continue to change. Each year as we prepare to travel, we become aware of students in our top groups who have never been out of Northern Indiana. The students in our program come from various backgrounds. We have students who are National Merit Finalists as well as extremely at-risk students who may not be excelling anywhere besides our program. We have students that come from affluent homes and students that can't even afford our $5.00/semester wardrobe fee. However, no students are ever excluded from a concert, trip, or other experience because they cannot afford to be involved.

The "secrets" to our continued success are based on some very simple principles to which we steadfastly adhere. The first is to make a plan. Goal setting is at the very center of what we do. As we approach each concert, musical, or trip, we plan carefully and stick to that plan. Part of planning is the understanding of what our goals are, what we hope to achieve, and what will be learned in the journey to the goal. Quite frankly, we plan to be excellent. We accept nothing less from our students, and they know it. If this means extra rehearsals, then that is what we do because we will not let them fail. Students' expectations for themselves and each other also are an important part of the accomplishment level we achieve each year. As we make our plans we recognize that if it doesn't sound exciting to us it will probably not be exciting to our students.

Our second principle is to model excellence for our students. We do not allow our students to coast, so neither do we. We continually raise the bar for ourselves as we raise the bar for the students. We demand excellence from ourselves in instruction, rehearsal, performance and vocal skills. We have found that it is important for our students not only to see us as teachers, but as excellent practitioners. We perform for them from time to time so they see not only can we teach, but also we can do. We work diligently at allowing our students to see us as learners just like they are. We are human to them…we laugh, cry, rant, praise, emote, and live fully in their presence. We enjoy the same from them.

The last principle is the quality of the journey for our students. As we work toward educational and performance goals, which go hand in hand for us, we are always concerned about means and the method. Our students know we work hard to make every class profitable. We accommodate many different learning styles and levels of talent in our program. Our students know we are not only interested in how well they perform but what they have learned on the way to the performance. Those areas of learning include music skills and styles, performance etiquette, poetic understanding, aesthetic perception, and joy in performance. Our grading program allows each student to define the types of activities in each nine weeks that best meet their musical growth needs.

For everything we achieve we make sure that our students reap the praise. The students do not see us as directors who stand in front, but rather as mentors guiding the way for the talented…and they are all talented. We work to make them believe in themselves as choral musicians. We also try to help them all feel they are important to our program. This takes a lot of energy and many after-school hours since there are over 215 students in our program each year. We make sure there are several opportunities throughout the year where we all sing together so each student feels a part of the whole. When our students leave us, many after four years of involvement, they feel a sense of accomplishment having been a part of the Goshen High School Choral Program.

    -MARCIA YOST

We asked the choir teacher what it takes to win a state championship. Her answer was not surprising. The music was introduced in a logical fashion, the difficult parts broken down into little pieces. Students worked hard at mastering the difficult music required to set themselves apart from all of the other schools in Indiana. There was not place for one student to sing off key. All had to be in perfect harmony. If the bass section had difficulty, they spent time with those bars of music until the rhythm or intonation would be corrected. How does this translate into the classroom? Don't all teachers want their students to be state champions as well? Of course, it is not that easy, but the logic is undeniable. We were on to something.

Step Three: From theory to practice

With 40 percent of our teachers benefiting from a daylong seminar aimed at understanding the concept of a learning model, obviously we were laying the groundwork for long-term focused staff development. Now that the core group had an understanding, it was time to do a shorter, but equally important foray into the learning model with the entire staff. The goal was to get each teacher to participate in a professional learning community sometime during the second semester of the year. In this learning community we would practice organizing a unit according to standards and assessing that unit for student learning. Actually, some groups liked the process of common planning so much that they decided to do common planning and assessment for the entire semester. Others were worried that there would be too many meetings and it would get in the way of teaching, but all agreed to give it a shot.

Again, when given the opportunity, teachers will come through. They really enjoyed the concept of essential learning and working together to plan units. It was not so enjoyable to analyze common assessments for student learning, but staff definitely saw the value of that exercise. We quietly learned that administrative monitoring is far simpler than monitoring student progress.

Staff development at this point is just the tip of the iceberg. What lies below the surface is a massive and powerful unknown. The challenge is to lift that iceberg further out of the water in the next few years. Centering all staff development on tweaking the three steps of the learning model provides the consistency and the content that teachers need to be more effective. Our promises were that the learning model would not be more work (it isn't) and that it would be successful (it is). Our students began to improve and we started to believe. We had suffered through what change gurus called the implementation dip and were at a point that our efforts resulted in student improvement.

The next phase of staff development now entails tailoring the learning model to individual teachers and professional learning communities. Below are broad examples of the three steps that have worked for many teachers at GHS:

Examples for essential learning
- **Student engagement**
- **Instructional strategies**
- **Writing in all classrooms**
- **Reading in content areas**
- **Managing the variety of cultures in schools**
- **Equity for all students**

Examples for assessing for student learning
- **Formative as opposed to summative assessment**
- **Technology for decision-making**
- **Looking into standards based assessments**

Examples for doing something about it
- **Finding more time**
- **Tutoring**
- **Resource time**
- **Increasing time for those needing additional help**
- **Writing grants**
- **Working individually with students**

We are not in a program nor are we looking for the answer. We are on a journey towards finding ways for all students to be successful. This journey puts the student at the center of all we do to create a personalized environment for each student.

Summary

The staff development program effectiveness should really be measured by the long-term impact on the classroom. Just as students are not all at one place, neither are teachers, so flexibility has to be built into the plan. Narrowing staff development to assist teachers with measuring the learning of students as a tool to impact instruction will pay dividends in student academic performance. The key is the administration must support and organize opportunities to improve instruction. Teachers, with the daily stress of preparing classes, soon lose sight of staff development efforts that do not move immediately into the regular school operation. For this reason, our school focuses on only two questions. What will make our students improve academically? How can we as teachers do our jobs better? Successfully answering of these questions will bring about change in how we do our work.

Chapter 4

Planning staff development without employing the learning model now reminds me of times in the classroom when the highest grade on a unit assessment was not very high at all. The feeling that I failed my students brought the big question, "What now?" Staff development can easily go in the same direction. If administrators expect teachers to use the learning model, why wouldn't they be held to the same standards? Taking time to assess the staff in their development saves more time in the long run. We learned this the hard way.

Getting Off Course

JIM KIRKTON, PRINCIPAL

We sat around the table after spending time in the spring and summer learning about a more organized way to observe what the instructional strengths and weaknesses of our teaching staff are. There was a level of excitement as we spent two days processing the strategy of "walk through" with professionals from our part of the state. We could hardly wait for all of our administrators to learn of its potential. Now we would be trained in how the students were participating in the learning process when we walked in the room. For years, we looked at any visit in the classroom as opportunity to see the teacher perform.

Based on my own experience as a pretty good performer, I recall kicking it into high gear on the rare occasions that an administrator actually showed up in my room. All of a sudden my energy level picked up, the discussion would become livelier, I was out among students more, and the visiting administrator could simply enjoy the dog and pony show. When the interloper disappeared, the scene would return to a more normal pace. Such was the state of classroom observations, particularly for those of us who were seasoned veterans.

Our entire team of administrators nodded when we discussed this educationally unique phenomenon. A new way of appearing for a short time out of nowhere certainly had appeal. We would check six different categories per visit, such as learning strategies, student involvement, grade level of instruction, the level of Bloom's Taxonomy, and use of appropriate materials. The beauty of the entire process was that teachers *knew what we were looking for*. They understood the levels of Blooms. They knew scores of instructional strategies. They wanted engaged students. All that was left was a study of the research-based best instructional strategies and

improving the quality of the assignments that would in turn improve the quality of students'
work as well.

A Plan is Born

How could we find the time to study the best instructional strategies? We knew that
merely listing them off would not work; too little information would do more damage than good.
As we discussed the lack of time and the need for information, we hatched a new approach. (Or,
I should say we hauled a previous approach out of the mothballs.) Our entire journey toward
becoming a professional learning community willing to talk about teaching and to share ideas
with each other came out of subdividing our staff into small groups for another book study.
Groups were random, but once again they met and shared and enjoyed the socialization. But this
time as a trade-off, we would no longer have staff meetings.

The suggestion was taking no more than one chapter per month. That would allow time
for experimentation with the instructional strategy between sessions. We really did not care
about the pacing of the book. As far as we were concerned they could take all year on one
chapter. Being students who had succeeded in the American education system themselves, they
all set out to do this project and learn from it. They especially appreciated the concession of not
having monthly staff meetings thus requiring no additional time.

Each spring, GHS and the local community honor all students with a 3.65 grade point
average at our academic honors banquet. The guest list includes the honored students, parents,
teachers selected by seniors, and community supporters. Hall of Fame inductions are also part of
the program. The number being recognized has grown as the focus on academic excellence has
grown. Our main challenge is finding a banquet hall large enough as the numbers have grown to
over 130 students and a banquet approaching 500. Students are given awards each year with
seniors earning a watch.
TED MAHNENSMITH—Assistant Principal

By November, I received reports that groups were having members miss their book study
sessions because they forgot. Thanksgiving even messed us up and Christmas would do the
same thing next month. Traditionally for the December staff meeting, we would have a staff
breakfast to celebrate our accomplishments. But not this year, because we had given up staff
meetings for more pertinent staff development, the book study.

I had said to our staff that school improvement comes from two levels. The first is
administrative organization. We had taken steps to improve scores through the professional

learning communities. We had found ways in our schedule to provide students with extra support they needed by provided tutoring and extra time in classrooms.

The second level was improving the impact of what we were doing in the classroom. Our course-alike groups had cooperatively refined their courses according to standards. This time provided more focused time in the classroom on the important standards and assisted with mutual accountability. Since many of our teachers were experienced and what I would consider very good teachers, this improvement would show up more slowly in our test scores.

Applying the Learning Model

When January and final exams became the next detractor from the book study, each administrator knew that the book study was on the ropes. We just never verbalized it. We all missed the monthly get together in our media center, mostly because we had always given gift certificates to recognize staff members for their accomplishments and we missed doing so. Plus we shares stories of our students, the real reasons we teach. As administrators we had embarked down a path for assisting the staff with learning. We had developed long term plans and were getting away from the "one shot" in-service. All of this should have been good, but it wasn't. This did not work for everybody because everybody was not at the same place.

We also had to assess the staff according to the learning model. Perhaps if we had openly discussed the book study earlier we might have gotten to the assessment sooner. As it was, in January we met with several staff members for two days to look at our entire school plan. These two days provide additional ammunition for the purpose of assessment in education. It is not about getting a grade, but finding information to impact instruction.

That night I went to my computer and sent out a staff email ending the book study. Was this a good move? Based on the response I received in the "Reply" column, the faculty concurred. They actually liked the staff meetings and felt they were important. When leading professionals towards a common vision, the collection of feedback is in important step. A protocol for any leader (teacher) to adhere to would be, "If someone has enough courage to come talk to me, then I should have the courage to listen." Over the years I have applied this motto to peers, all levels of staff, parents, community, and students. Sometimes they are wrong or their fears are misplaced, but usually this feedback provides important and strategic information. Getting beyond defensiveness—offering the speaker a chance to air concerns—is extremely important. The real reinforcement in this process comes when the administrator acts upon the recommendation of the courageous person who came forwards.

G/T program

As public education is pushed further into standardized curriculum and standardized testing, teachers and students struggle with ensuring all students grow and find school challenging and rewarding. This struggle is even more true for teachers of gifted and talented students.

In my English 9 Gifted and Talented class, the curriculum is accelerated and more enriched. All of the material (units) that the other 9th grade classes teach is taught, as well as three additional units.

- Short Stories (This unit occurs around the ISTEP testing)
- **The Odyssey**
- Non-fiction
- Poetry
- **Romeo and Juliet**
- **To Kill a Mockingbird**
- **The Hunchback of Notre Dame (GT only)**
- **The Count of Monte Cristo (GT only)**
- **Fahrenheit 451 (GT only)**
    * Grammar is taught throughout the year. Writing is part of each unit. Students are required to read four approved outside books and complete assignments on them before the end of the year.

Unlike most of the other 9th grade classes, I have these same students for the entire year. We focus almost entirely on the higher level of Bloom's Taxonomy. Each unit is more in-depth and rigorous for the gifted students. For instance, they must be able to not only identify a Sonnet, but they must be able to count the iambic pentameter and tell if the poet has strayed from the meter or rhyme and what effect that may cause. For each unit, students are given traditional and non-traditional assessments. At the end of each semester, students must complete a culminating project that demonstrates understanding.

One of the greatest challenges is finding out what they don't know. GT students pride themselves on knowing. And there is always that one student who might. However, in the understanding of backward design curriculum, my job is to find a way to measure where they are and find a way to where the need to get. I use all of the scores (M.A.P.S., ISTEP, and lexiles) and spend most of the first unit (Short Stories) finding their individual strengths and weaknesses. This information, along with the Indiana State Academic Standards, helps me set goals for the class. Having the same students all year allows me to adjust the goals and share with them the growth I see.

The Gifted / Talented students are unlike other classes because the majority of these students have been in the same classes since the fourth grade. When they come to the high school, they often look forward to my class where they are sure to see each other.

Besides evaluating them academically, I consider them socially. Often G/T students have social and emotional issues, and although these students are academically gifted, they are not all "teacher pleasers." I work to know each one of these students and his or her individual needs.
JAIME SHREINER

Doing something about assessment

Unilaterally we ended the book study and returned to team building. But our administrative team also saw a need to make assessment of learning much more transparent in our own facilitation of staff development. Our certified teaching staff is currently composed of approximately 85 teachers and supported by collaborators in the ENL department and paraprofessionals in the special needs areas, though each year we have certain staff turnover for which we had not earlier accommodated. At the time of this publication, we have been on the learning model journey for the past four years, but in each of those years, new personalities have been added into the mix.

New certified staff members were assigned mentors to assist in induction, but we had concerns about just how comfortable our new (and even some of our experienced) teachers were in understanding and implementing the learning model in the classroom.

We moved ahead with our staff development plans and created consternation and maybe some separation. It was time to get back on the same page, or should I say, it was time to get to the page of each staff member. We created a large banner exhibiting five levels of comfort with the three questions of the learning model in order to get some feedback from the staff.

- **Level One—Not sure what the learning model is or how to use it**
- **Level Two—Understand the learning model but not using it in my classroom or course alike**
- **Level Three—Understand the learning model and used it to plan with course alike group**
- **Level Four-- Understand the learning model and use assessments to check instruction to some level**
- **Level Five—Learning model is fully integrated into how my classroom operates.**

Each teacher was given a sticky note. On the back of this sticky note, we instructed them to place their names and the letter "L" if they wanted to be leaders. It did not matter where they were on the chart regarding the learning model for the "L" because we just wanted to be able to identify staff member who might be willing to step forth.

The results of this survey surprised us very little. We had set too quick a pace, moving onto the next step before fully understanding the last one. The visual of the sticky notes on the banner revealed teachers in all areas of understanding. Understandably, most teachers at Level 1 had been hired in the last couple of years. A significant number of teachers were in the middle and finding it difficult to move on the "assessment and doing something about it."

With this information, we could now be more focused in planning future staff development. Originally we took an entire day to help some teachers understand the common sense of the learning model. But we had not done that with the entire staff, including the newer teachers. The entire staff was not ready to look at instructional strategies as we had assumed. We planned in detail the next steps in helping all teachers move up the continuum toward Level 5. At the writing of this book, this journey is barely under way, but it feels more purposeful and individualized. Of course, we will do some large group celebration, but the growth of our staff will have to be more individualized in the future if we hope to continue our momentum. The teachers have been good team members, but they will only come to practice if the practice works on the skills they have. There is no point in practicing game-winning shots from half court when some members are still learning the rules of the game.

Summary

The learning model is really a simple model that can and should be used at all levels of decision-making. As building administrators it calls us to look at each and every step we take in staff training. Administrators and school districts must model the process for it to benefit all. As we have become more familiar with gathering and utilizing data, our decisions can be more informed rather than intuitive. Along the way, there will be missteps or misjudgments. Conversations with our staff and paying close attention to the information gathered are important parts of assessing and doing something about the plan. School and academic growth are not the products of one person or one department. Growth is the responsibility of all.

Chapter 5

While there really is no simple way for schools to move toward academic improvement, those that have been successful have focused efforts on two fronts. The first is student academic performance, and the learning model grows from this effort. The second deals with the improving performance of teachers through effective and focused staff development. This entire book could be written on staff development and would be like any of the hundreds written on the topic, but for us success has come from the marriage of improving student performance and teacher skills. For students to flourish, they must attend a school that is tuned to their needs and which follows their individual progress. We have adopted the term of "School of One" as the standard motto for our behavior and decision-making. The learning model provides constant assessment and the forum to discuss change.

School of One

JIM KIRKTON, PHIL LEDERACH, CHRIS WEAVER AND THE SRT COMMITTEE

Ten years ago, prior to the current administrator, Goshen High School teachers and administrators embarked on a challenging course to be the first Indiana school to earn the high level accreditation from North Central Association (NCA) called a transitions endorsement. This required the school basically to track and document the progress of each student in reading, writing, problem solving, career awareness, and employability skills. When our staff began this, there were constant challenges. The teachers had difficulty defining a range of success in these areas, let alone measuring each student in them. For example, how do you measure and document employability skills? The only constant and pertinent measurements were tardies and absences. However, studies have shown that school attendance patterns may have little to do with actual attendance in the work place. In fact, many students with poor attendance often become prompt and dependable at work, mostly because attending work has literal value in the form of paychecks. Then we still had to find two other indicators of student success besides the untrustworthy attendance record.

State accreditation required triangulated data in all areas, with some type of benchmark to determine if students would be credentialed or not. In the end, homeroom teachers were given some rubric type guidelines to plug in the students' information. Afterward, the teacher would need to label the student as credentialed or not credentialed.

As can be imagined, this turned out to be a monumental process. When it was all completed, the information showed us that the students we labeled as credentialed matched very closely with the pass rate for the Graduation Qualifying Exam. Too much work, in other words, to tell us what we already knew.

Theatre for One

We are to build a school of one. It is a process that perhaps we will never finish completely. Each year and each student present a new challenge. But we can look a student in the eye and say truthfully, "Our school provides resources for you."

How do the arts, particularly theatre, help this process? Theatre is a resource. Engagement has always been the key to successful learning. Engaging students in a production, which is more important than their role in the production, creates a shared goal of a respected, well-received production. There will never be a perfect performance. There is always the challenge of improving. In the process of producing a piece of drama, the students are actively pursuing the goal of improvement to motivate them to their best. This is the same attitude GHS has towards overcoming challenges. "We can do better," but it is always a process.

Theatre can epitomize a smaller learning community in this way. The shared goal is the key to learning. Having students work as a team towards a goal makes leading them easier. This is true onstage, in rehearsal, and in the classroom. We know what we want to know. We share the objective. We bring the entire cast or classroom to the understanding. We share the process. A small learning community, a cast, a class, reads for understanding, discusses for clarification and debates interpretation. They become a unit of learners, a school of one.

Goshen High School is diverse, and theater is inclusive. This is important; a school of one must include all. Regardless of how many students who are seen onstage, there are many more involved. As a theatre educator I have yet to turn down a student who volunteers to work. Students want to be part of the process and own the product.

"A school of one" is fundamentally about not letting any student slip by, fall through the cracks. The more we get these students involved the better. Theatre is just part of the many diverse activities that are opportunities for student at GHS. Theatre is a resource for many students, the one place a student may fit in. GHS is and always should be in the process of creating a school of one, a place where educators have the resources to help students become involved.

-RICHARD P. SNYDER

For students who were not credentialed but had no time for the process—for example, a student who transferred to Goshen as a senior—we were to help them gain the proper credentials in key areas. This sounded very good, but we were having difficulty explaining to students *why* they needed to be credentialed. The information would not show up on transcripts or diplomas. Neither colleges nor the workplace would know what the term "credentialing" meant or even know the student's character based on the results. The top students had the most questions, and they were the ones who most vehemently questioned the validity of going through this process without some type of reward in the end.

We knew that the yearly exercise of gathering information on students and creating charts for credentialing would soon be become another one of the passing educational fads. When applying the learning model to the credentialing form, it was obvious the information gathered was not being used for student improvement. The call went to the state director of NCA to inform him that we would soon be dropping their top accreditation. The exercise, while interesting, was not providing us with information we needed to do our jobs.

In actuality, we were heading down a different road, attempting to create a sense of a smaller learning environment toward a "School of One." And for this road we had clear goal areas outline by the Smaller Learning Community grant:

Smaller Learning Community Goals

1. **To insure that all students graduate with the knowledge and skills necessary to make successful transitions to college and careers.**

2. **To improve academic rigor and student achievement.**

3. **To enhance the school climate.**

4. **To create personalized environments for learning and teaching.**

In the fall we had started weekly grade and attendance checks distributed to homeroom teachers on an easily accessible Excel spreadsheet. These teachers can access the information on their desktops each week and know if students were rising or falling.

It is becoming better known in education that interventions for faltering students must be put in place within three weeks. This is commonly called the 15-day window. Our plan for the homeroom Student Resource Time was to monitor student progress weekly to assist getting necessary help to students as soon as possible. Currently, each week students attend 180 minutes of resource time (two 90 minute periods) that can be used for study, tutoring, mentoring, and make-up. Each student has at least one teacher in the building checking on him/her every week. In other words, all students have at least one adult that will make every effort to not let them fail. The School of One in action.

The following chart shows the information provided to SRT teachers each week to enable them to monitor progress of students. The weekly information is critical for students and their advisors in the discussion of academic progress and for setting up possible interventions. These are actual scores with names changed. Students are divided by bold letters. The second student, William, is destined for some serious intervention spearheaded by the counselor and the student's SRT teacher. But this chart shows more than who is not passing, it tells the story of the student progress through school and provides a centerpiece for conversation on a weekly basis. It is interesting to note on that the student failing four classes has an improving grade in French. This information shows us that the French teacher may have some insight into this student or has connected in some way. This information may help us recover this student—one who used to be left to flounder on his own.

First	Class	14-Sep	Mid-Term	27-Sep	27-Sep
Robert	**Geometry - H**	**A**	**A**	**A**	**90%**
Robert	**Media Arts II**	**Blank**	**B**	**B**	**88%**
Robert	**Economics**	**D**	**D+**	**D+**	**68%**
Robert	**Adult Roles & Resp.**	**A**	**A**	**A**	**96%**
Robert	**Expository Writing**		**A**	**B**	**B**
Robert	**Ceramics I**	**F**	**F**	**D**	**86%**
Robert	**Physical Dev. II**	**B**	**B+**	**B+**	**66%**
William	Algebra I	D	F	F	**90%**
William	Biology	C+	F	F	59%
William	English 9	D-	F	F	50%
William	Health Education	F	F	F	42%
William	Phys. Education I	A	B+	B	55%
William	French I	D	D	C	85%
Mario	**Adv. Crimson Jazz**	**Blank**	**A**	**A**	73%
Mario	**Concert Band**	**Blank**	**A**	**A**	99%
Mario	**Eng Lan/Comp W131 AP**	**C**	**B**	**B**	97%
Mario	**Pre Calculus-H**	**B**	**B**	**B**	86%
Mario	**US History**	**B-**	**B-**	**A**	78%
Mario	**Bio II-Genet/Ethics**	**Blank**	**B**	**B**	97%
Mario	**Phys. Education I**	**A**	**A**	**A**	85%
Chelsea	Contemp. Lit - H	C	C	C	**97%**
Chelsea	Algebra II-H	C	C	C	76%
Chelsea	German III	A	A	A	65%
Chelsea	Media Arts I	Blank	A	A	92%
Chelsea	Spanish I	A	B+	B	92%
Chelsea	US History	B-	B-	A-	86%

Chelsea	Physics I	B-	B+	B	92%
Brittany	**Algebra II**	**F**	**C**	**C**	87%
Brittany	**Media Arts I**	**Blank**	**A**	**A**	72%
Brittany	**Physics I**	**B+**	**B**	**B**	93%
Brittany	**Spanish III**	**B**	**B+**	**B-**	85%

The SRT teacher can easily see the progress of the student from week to week to determine student productivity in the class. Also included in the spreadsheet is the attendance even though it is not provided on this sample. The SRT teacher, and any teacher for that matter, can sort this information to quickly access desired information.

Student Resource Time (SRT)

Student Resource Time and its functions are complex, but they are also highlights of what we do for our students. This flexible time has increased the number of students performing at the honor roll level and has reduced student failure relative to our increased rigor in our curriculum. This period provides the needed extra time outside of class that some students must have to master the materials. The tutoring portion also allows for help from different teachers or from peers. The entire concept of Student Resource Time hatched from our belief that all students will learn if given enough time.

**Note
Our plan calls for improving student performance and teacher effectiveness.
In order to reach our goals, we focus efforts in two areas:

SCHOOL OF ONE (SRT)
- Forming strong relationships with students
- Improving student learning

PROFESSIONAL LEARNING COMMUNITIES
- Course-alike groups
- Other Professional Learning Community opportunities

This extra time can be structured for individual students. Teachers can communicate among themselves to assure that students make the best use of the time allotted. For example, an absent student may miss an English quiz and a biology lab in one day. In the past, that student would have had to spend those class periods on Tuesday to make up work, in effect missing two classes for one absence. Plus, before or after school make-up times are rarely possible make-up times for students from poverty who depend on the school bus for transportation. In this, we see again that the educational system consistently tilts in favor of middle- and upper-class students who have available transportation, while students who may need the most help continue to get locked out.

Enhancing School of One through North Central Association

Our School of One concept, upon investigation, is not much different from the transitions endorsement provided through NCA. The difference is that in our case, we were generating the information we needed about our students, while with the transitions model, we were trying to meet their requirements. There is a giant chasm between the two.

Letter from a parent about having a student feel included.
    I wanted to tell you what a positive influence band has been on Brian. Brian has struggled alot finding something that he loves to do. Band has been the answer. He loves to play trumpet, he loved the marching band and the competitions. He is learning to be disciplined and responsible also, Words cannot express how much this means to us as his parents. He struggles in school and until band had not found his "nitch." He has made friends in band that are good influences on him. As his parents we want to thank you for your part in making the Goshen High School band a great thing.
TOM COX—Band Director

In meeting with our state director for NCA, we outlined our concerns about the load of paperwork required through their guidelines. At the same time we shared how we felt our path very closely paralleled their expectations. The difference really came down to how we perceived the final product. Our contention was that our students would perform better academically if we use the learning model as our *modus operandi*. NCA agreed and offered us more flexibility. In return we offered to be transparent in what all we do. We are not a research institution; we are practitioners. We will learn only by working with other practitioners either in our school or in other schools. Teachers at GHS work with peers in course-alike; within the Northern Lakes

Conference we work with other schools for curriculum and assessment; and within our state we work with other schools so that we can continue learning and have objective views about our progress.

The School of One Takes Hold

The School of One is only a natural progression based on how our staff labeled itself. The following is the vision, and while visions often do not play a significant role in how a school behaves, in our case the vision is being realized step by step.

Goshen High School Vision

A. Student Performance
1. Students are actively engaged in learning
2. Students value school
3. Students have strong school involvement both in and out of the classroom

B. Instruction
1. Teachers are highly competent and passionate about subject matter valuing learning over grades
2. Teachers direct classrooms that are goal oriented and measured
3. Teachers use reading as central to learning

C. Climate
1. School community cares about students and teachers in all ways
2. School recognizes student and teacher accomplishments
3. School provides a safe environment
4. School provides a positive social environment

D. Community
1. The community recognizes the excellence of the school
2. The community sees diversity as a strength
3. The community cooperates in educational process with parents, staff, and students

Next we refined the purpose of SRT even further with yearly topics to cover with students. Each year students require help with certain transitional issues. Below are the two goals our staff focuses on during SRT, plus a few procedures.

Goal #1: SRT teachers will set the tone so that students understand that academic progress and success are expected.

- SRT teachers will take attendance within the first 10 minutes and make sure students are where they are assigned.
- SRT teachers will create an atmosphere that is conducive to studying.
- SRT teachers will check students' grades, attendance, etc. weekly.
- SRT teachers will initiate and document academic interventions when needed.
- SRT teachers will use the credentialing process to monitor student progress and to help the student with academic planning.

Goal #2: SRT teachers will know each student personally, creating a "school of one".
- SRT teachers will make referrals to appropriate school-based resources (guidance counselor, school nurse, STAT, etc.) when needed.
- In addition to monitoring academic progress, SRT teachers will encourage and monitor involvement in school activities.
- SRT teachers will assist students with school business (scheduling, career planning, goal-setting, etc.).

Below are some areas for discussion with all students either as a group or individually. This list is supplemented each year as guidance surveys, local surveys, and other school related tasks are required. At the end of four years together with these discussion topics, the SRT teacher and the student will have had some valuable conversations.

Freshman year:
- New school policies
- Finding services within the building (guidance, athletics, music, etc.)
- Preparation for the GQE
- NWEA testing
- State ISTEP+ testing
- Scheduling and selecting classes
- Media services
- Technology
- After Hours program
- Graduation requirements
- Time management and study skills
- Preparing for final exams
- Transcripts
- Participating in school activities
- Driver education and summer school
- Remediation programs based on test results
- Specified guidance needs
- School involvement
- Goal setting

Sophomore year:

- Scheduling and course selection
- PSAT and SAT preparation
- Study skills
- Career center program and job skills
- Mentorship and internship possibilities
- Summer School
- Preparation for GQE test
- Remediation for GQE test
- Initial exposure to colleges and college requirements
- Class and school activities
- Specified guidance needs
- School involvement
- Goal setting

Junior year:

- PSAT and SAT test preparation
- Scheduling and course selection (increased rigor)
- College and career guidance and instruction
- Mentorship and internship possibilities
- Summer School
- Remediation for GQE if needed
- Specified guidance needs
- School involvement
- Goal setting

Senior year:

- SAT test preparation
- College and career encouragement and support
- Remediation for GQE if needed
- Specified guidance needs
- Goal setting
- School involvement
- Final check for graduation

Even though the list grows smaller every year, the potential for conversation between teacher and students actually increases each year as SRT teachers get to know their students better. This conversation, coupled with weekly updates on academic performance and attendance, keeps each student directly in the sights of the SRT teacher. Arriving at this point with a diverse staff takes time, focus, and effort on the part of everyone in the building. But still, each year we must re-apply the learning model to our actions in order to make sure we are still headed in the right direction.

Summary

A staff must work together to create a personalized learning environment for students. No longer can we afford to disappear into our rooms and teach in perpetual solitude. The learning model provides a method for looking at everything we do. If it helps our students know exactly what they must learn (and it does), then it also helps our staff know what we expect of ourselves. By working with organizations like NCA and defining the expectations for the School of One, teachers are free to focus on what is important. For example, SRT provides more academic time for students and supports the teacher in the classroom, but it also provides an avenue of communication between teacher and student, creating a personalized sense for students. We are a long way from perfect or even good at this, but our steps are making inroads.

Chapter 6

Our school graduation rate has been as low as 60% and never had risen above the low 70's. There just are too many students that have struggles with the traditional school setting. The school corporation had contracted with an outside agency to provide alternative education services. But, our numbers were capped at 30 at any given time and we figured that we had at least 120 students needing this type of placement. After two years of study we opened our own alternative school with the curriculum provided by NovaNet. Immediately we found success changing the atmosphere of our school while keeping more students in school. The graduation rate rose into the 80's and eventually topped 90% in a couple of years. This program, like all initiatives, is under constant assessment and revision, but has become an integral part of what we do. The staff is dedicated to assisting students to achieve their goals in an alternative setting.

Merit Learning Center (Alternative School)

BOB EVANS, PRINCIPAL OF MERIT LEARNING CENTER

Merit Learning Center seeks out students who may or most likely may not experience success. Students come to Merit with a desire to salvage their high school efforts and a hope that they may attend school again and graduate.

Several high schools have emphasized that they see Merit as a privilege for students to attend. Those students who are not fully availing themselves of the opportunities at Merit are often reminded that they must perform or may be replaced by other students on the waiting list to enroll.

Merit Learning Center has evolved from a single modular trailer serving one school into a full-time program for six corporations within Elkhart County. Each district in the co-op (Baugo, Concord, Fairfield, Goshen, Middlebury, and WaNee) sets its own sending criteria for students who may attend. Some schools identify students with poor attendance or disruptive behavior. But schools that select students based on their needs for an alternative educational setting find

While showing a visiting team of administrators around the school, I stepped into a lab where 45 students were quietly engaged in their work. I asked, "Would any of you like to go back to your sending school?"... Not one hand was raised.

the most success. With the focus on creating a positive environment, Merit Center does not accept students who have been expelled, but does accept students as an alternative to expulsion.

Once a student has been selected to attend Merit, the registration process at the sending school begins with parental involvement and a transfer of records that includes testing information, grades, transcript analysis, and any other pertinent information. The six school corporations maintain enrollment of their students and send them to Merit as a satellite program of their own campus. Students are told that Merit should be seen as a long hallway connected to their sending schools, but that offers more options and flexibility, as well as accountability.

Tiffany: A bright mother of a toddler with older siblings who were very successful in high school academics, sports and extracurriculars. Her parents were very embarrassed and frustrated over her pregnancy, but remained supportive of their daughter. Tiffany focused on being a very attentive mother, and determined to work hard academically. She finished high school in three years. At the time she had no idea that she could meet the qualifications for graduating early. She is now enrolled at a local college working towards a degree in business administration/management major. She and her family were absolutely thrilled with her successes at Merit and her graduation in June of 2005 as a Core 40 student.
—RUTH COMSTOCK, COUNSELOR

Resources of the six districts have enabled Merit occupy and refurbish the Riverdale Elementary School building to accommodate high-speed internet and video conferencing capabilities for 70 new networked computers. As a result, enrollment capacity has grown from 120 students to 275.

Merit employs licensed teachers in science, math, English, social studies, special needs, and K-12 physical education/health. The support staff includes a full-time guidance counselor, job coach, secretary, and four instructional assistants. Teachers present the curriculum in ways that build connections for students who lack internal motivation and they are also responsible for development of coursework within their content areas. However, Merit's teachers also seek cross-curricular integration. Additional curricular assistance is available from Goshen High School through teacher mentorships. Merit provides a positive learning environment that meets students uniquely at their individual levels. The certified teachers in English, math, science, and social studies act as lead teachers for both online and offline work in their curricular areas. The full-time counselor, job coach, special education teacher, and a K-12 teacher provide additional cross-curricular academic support.

Jonathon: Was a 5th year senior. His sending school was extremely concerned that he would never graduate. They'd seen him fall short of meeting expectations so many times. It looked like he wasn't going to survive even the first few weeks of the academic year. Jonathon had panic attacks, deep depressive cycles with verbalized intentions of taking his own life, and spells of intense physical illness. Further, he was kicked out of his apartment and also his grandmother's house where he'd attempted refuge on several occasions. Jonathon had huge unresolved grief and loss issues. Merit worked with his medical doctor and staff. He received a tremendous amount of encouragement and educational support from the staff at Merit on a daily basis. His sending school had created a deadline beyond which they would discontinue paying for his slot at Merit. We all held our breath, but Jonathon was allowed to earn his last credit a

day after the deadline. He was beaming with success on his last day as he hugged those who had mentored him throughout his experience at Merit.
-- RUTH COMSTOCK--COUNSELOR

During Merit's first year as a countywide school, approximately 20% of the students enrolled were identified for special education services. In those cases, the Merit staff held conferences to re-write Individual Education Plans (IEP) for special needs or Individualized Learning Plans (ILP) for English Language Learners. During the students' first week, with the conference review being slated for one year from that date. Quite often there is a struggle to find the best academic fit for these students; online independent study and large amounts of reading rarely match well with student needs. The special education teacher works diligently to find alternative curricular delivery methods, though even this process does not always ensure the desired level of success. Ultimately, it was decided that students should be able to read at a 5th grade level to enroll at Merit. However, we continue to work with students and the abilities they have.

Janet made a commitment to her daughter who was a senior at Goshen High School. If her daughter would work hard to earn the credits she needed for graduation then mom would also work to earn the high school diploma she never had. Merit offered her the flexibility and support to do just that. Janet worked diligently, missed an extended period of time due to illness, but toward the end of the year was spending 8-10 hours a day to meet her goals. With four days until graduation, Janet had earned the last of the 10 credits she needed. An exuberant Janet left Merit with a pride that had evaded her for decades.

All students exit the program when they have met specific goals, graduated, or when a sending school agrees it is in the student's best interest to return. Until then, we endeavor to meet their needs.

Each student leaving Merit, either to return to their sending school or in transitioning to life, works his/her way through an exit interview procedure with our guidance counselor to assist in establishing career goals and/or post-secondary plans.

Course curriculum at Merit is a mixture of online tutorials and offline project-based curriculum. The purpose of this nontraditional educational environment is to assist students in earning a diploma, thereby enhancing opportunities for job-advancement or postsecondary schooling. The general curriculum base at Merit is contained in two online prescriptive instructional programs that pretest concepts and design lessons to assist students in achieving mastery. All teachers work to ensure that the curriculum is aligned to Indiana standards. These programs then free teachers to focus on either intense one-on-one remediation or more creative lessons that involve project-based, collaborative teamwork. Curriculum revisions have emphasized more links to career interests as well as integrating writing across the scope of a student's curricular needs. Even though our goal has been to connect all students, our assessment is that we have fallen short of our goal of building connections for all students. We continue to emphasize student tracking of standards achievement as well as job skills and career education as a goal for Merit.

An old building that once housed Riverdale Elementary School is home to Merit and two preschool programs. These preschool programs offer Merit students the opportunity for service learning and mentorships. Students attend classes then walk down the hall to assist the preschool teachers.

Each teacher at Merit adheres to instructional objectives that dictate learning methods. The two online components are intertwined to balance and supplement each other. Larger group instruction is used minimally but continues to be developed, including lessons using Power Point and Web Quest models of instruction that are then individualized per students' interests. Small groups of students may be formed to participate in collaborative, hands-on projects related to the students' career interests. Linking the curriculum to information gained from another online career oriented program has become a vital component of making school relevant for students.

Merit is committed to not only academics, but also to lifelong learning that will help students become productive and confident members of their community. Every student enrolled at Merit is assigned a job skills course as an elective credit. Components of this course include writing resumes and letters of introduction as well as identification and personalization of skills needed to function well in society: interviewing skills, communication skills, and interpersonal relationships. When linked to information from college- and career-related tutorials, educational goals can then be connected to each student's curriculum choices, forming individualized learning plans. Staff at Merit believe that the marriage of these components provide the best options for meeting the needs of each student.

Stated simply, technology is an integral part of Elkhart County Merit Learning Center. Merit uses the Internet in transitioning and managing student information.

Merit Learning Center has been recognized as an exemplary alternative school by the Indiana State Department of Education.

An enrollment template containing each student's background and academic needs is prepared by the sending school and then transmitted via e-mail to Merit. This template is combined with documents pertaining to standardized testing, reasons the student was sent to an alt/ed site, transcript analysis, the student's short and long-term goals as well as information gleaned from the college and career on-line programs to form an IEP or ILP. The student management system used by Merit has been set-up to enable personnel at each sending school to act as homeroom teachers for their students via the Internet. Each school then has access to attendance, academics, and teacher notes pertaining to their students.

Some students with very low reading levels have been placed at Merit, with little academic success. Merit discourages enrollment for students with less than a 5th grade reading level. Students with low reading levels are unlikely to have success with on-line curriculum. Further intake guidelines will be developed and shared with sending schools.

Merit accepts students at the discretion of the sending schools. Each sending school designates students being sent to Merit into one of six categories:

- Student intends to withdraw or has withdrawn before graduation
- Student has not complied academically and would benefit from alternative instruction
- Student is a parent or an expectant parent unable to regularly attend traditional school
- Student is a disruptive student
- Student is employed and employment is necessary to support student or family
- Student is post-high school age, but desires to earn high school diploma

These designations appear on the enrollment form and provide Merit's guidance counselor valuable information for each student entering the program. Upon entering Merit Center, an intake conference is held with the guidance counselor to analyze transcripts, hear concerns from parents and students, and assist the student in defining short- and long-term goals. Following this, individual and small group orientation to the building prepares students for the transition to Merit. Next students are assigned to one of four possible sessions based upon their needs and the availability of the program. Lastly, each student is introduced to his/her case manager, usually the session teacher.

Teachers rotate throughout all sessions every week, giving students the benefit a consistent teacher as well as individual assistance in specific academic areas. Teachers are assigned to certain groups of students and track the academic performance, attendance, social issues, and behavioral issues of those students. The interpersonal relationships established through case management are the key to building links between the students and school. Without this link, many students would dropout of a school they see as meaningless.

A Web-based student management system is used by Merit teachers to log case management notes for students.

Subject-area teachers complement the case manager by designing and assessing offline curriculum to fill potential gaps left by computer-assisted instruction. As stated above, a job coach has been added to the program to assist students in maintaining local part-time jobs or adding service to students' school schedules. In case of behavior problems, intervention plans are developed for each student, based on reported observations or anecdotal evidence on why the student has not experienced success at the sending school.

Final exams from Goshen High School are used to add credibility to student performance.

Logistically, Merit operates four sessions throughout the day, and recommends that all students have jobs or perform service-learning projects for credit through its Youth Potential Program (YPP) to complete the other half of their daily educational requirements. To further augment student needs, Merit also offers assistance to students currently working in a traditional high school schedule to take a single class through Merit to recover credits or to take classes in such areas as reading, standardized testing remediation, and SAT/ACT preparation.

Grade reporting when working towards mastery - Whenever students finish a class, they receive credit notifications to take home. Our overriding philosophy is to create an environment where student needs and academic standards are merged to create success. At any time parents can request a course-by-course update from Merit.

Average daily attendance for the first year of the cooperative was approximately 80 percent. Absent students received calls each day, building the relationship between students' families and the staff. Merit averaged about two students per enrollment slot during the first year of the cooperative. These students typically did not attend their high schools and were given the option of attending Merit. School had not been a place of success for them and it seems that they did not give Merit the opportunity to change that perception. The majority of absences, and Merit's turnover rate, can be largely attributed to students who attended Merit less than 15 days. Those who we were able to connect during that initial time tended to be productive. Our focus for the coming year is to provide a more of a multifaceted safety net by teachers, counselor, job coach, and others towards effective support for students who have already given up on school when they are assigned to Merit.

Students who are working and attending to Merit are very busy people. Many students work between 30 and 40 hours a week in addition to their classes at Merit and some have additional responsibilities as parents. A vision we have for the school-to-work program (YPP) is to develop a core group of employers in the community who will contact us here at Merit when they have open positions, so that Merit becomes an integral part of the hiring and evaluation process. In this manner, we will be able to tie in school attendance with job attendance so that students can earn high school credits while working. Hopefully this will encourage students to stay in school until they graduate.

Best Practice Instructional Strategies include, but may not be limited to:
- Computer assisted instruction; immediate feedback
- Faster teacher feedback
- Case-management system assists teachers in building personal relationships with students.
- Small group and one-on-one instruction
- Student choice in what core areas are being worked on (within SIP)
- Reduced schedules with no "frill" such as passing period help students focus
- Short lessons, both online and offline
- Long-term projects that are designed in manageable chunks.
- Internet provides base for research
- Students receive individual attention in computer graphics and presentations
- Resume workshop is small group and/or one-on-one; focuses student attention on self-awareness of their personal qualities of excellence
- Whole-school service-learning projects
- Credits available through both YPP jobs and service learning opportunities

Students have daily interaction with Head Start and special needs' preschool children.

Getting Out into the Building with
The Learning Model and the School of One

Chapter 7

Finding ways for students to transition successfully from middle school to high school is a continual challenge for all schools. Looking at academic data about our 9th graders made this even more evident. Not all freshmen have the same adjustment issues, and therefore a single plan would not work for all students. We decided to identify students with specific academic needs and address them through a variety of means. Our main premise is that the freshman year is a critical time for students. The key for us is in the planning and preparation using the data that is available to make the best decisions possible.

Freshman Initiatives

PHIL LEDERACH, ASSISTANT PRINCIPAL

The Obstacles and Challenges

Our intuition told us that even though we had a good school, we had a problem with freshmen at Goshen High School. We didn't know exactly what caused it, but we did know that we were spending time and effort on our freshmen and, in many cases, were not getting what we hoped in return. Our first step was to identify the problem, so we started gathering the data. It did not take long for the numbers to tell us that our intuition was right: We had some serious issues with our freshmen.

That is not startling news to anyone who works in a high school. In fact, nationwide, high school freshmen account for a disproportionate number of truancies, tardies, behavioral issues, suspensions, expulsions, and failures to earn credit. Our data showed us that Goshen High School freshmen in the 2002-2003 school year were no different than most high schools. Our ninth graders accounted for:

- 43% of all truancies
- 50% of all cheating infractions
- 45% of all inappropriate behavior infractions

- 51% of all insubordination infractions
- 54% of all fighting infractions
- 40% of all detentions assigned
- 57% of all gang-related infractions
- 66% of all busing probations
- 46% of all in-house suspensions
- 52% of all out of school suspensions

Those darn freshmen—and please note the restraint here. Every time we turned around, we were dealing with a freshman going into crisis, disappearing from a class, getting in a fight, or perhaps most frustrating, just refusing to do what normal humans take for granted as normal behavior. *Normal human* may be an oxymoron, and especially so when applied to high school freshmen, but clearly many of our freshmen were not having the academic or social successes that we expected. To compound the frustrations with freshmen, we discovered that an inordinate number of our ninth graders were not only failing to comply to school rules and norms, they were literally failing, and doing so at a much higher rate than their upperclassmen peers. In fact, on our first F-Lists (we tracked students with failing grades), we discovered that many more freshmen were failing classes than sophomores, and freshmen were failing at almost twice the rate of juniors and seniors. This did not, however, mean that every freshman was having problems, but comparatively, freshmen were having more difficulties than the students in grades 10-12.

Knowledge changes perspectives. As educators we know and believe this to be true. It is not always a pleasant experience, however, if we are the ones that have to do the changing. After collecting the preliminary numbers, we knew we could not continue as we had, hoping that these unruly freshmen would matriculate to stubborn sophomores, morph into somewhat compliant juniors, and blossom into mature and articulate seniors for at least one semester—until senioritis kicked in and they reverted back to patterns established in their freshmen year, but usually tempered by good humor and mutual respect on the parts of both the seniors and the staff.

While standing in the commons area during parent teacher conferences, students attending IVY Tech, a local community college, were entering as they headed for their classes. It is great to have a building with parents entering to talk with teachers, and community members entering to attend college or adult level classes. Each term we have about 300 adult students enrolled in college classes and another 100 enrolled in English as a Second Language classes. While greeting all who entered, a former student of Mr. Lederach's entered and came over to talk to him. This student was recalling the senior project required in Mr. Lederach's English class. This student was not a strong student, but he had been given an opportunity to explore an area of interest for research, model airplanes. For his presentation, they went out on the football field and he demonstrated flying his airplane.

Following this demonstration, several of the students must have complimented him on his presentation because he was actively recounting the details of that day. Mr. Lederach later commented that this student would have a difficult time graduating with today's standards. Yet, here he was, dropping his wife off for college classes, working in the community, and raising a young family. He was feeling that his life was good. One of the reasons for this was that a teacher, Mr. Lederach, took the time to get to know this student and then provided a means for the student to share his passions.

Stories like these are why schools have to find opportunities for all students. This daunting task is absolutely necessary for the futures of our students. All the testing in the world will not make lives better. What will make lives better are teachers/mentors that work with students and help them to uncover their passions opening the door to becoming productive citizens. The call is to build a School of One where every student feels noticed and valued.
Jim Kirkton

Something had to change, but we wanted to be very careful about our changes because we also knew that we were doing quite a few things right. Most freshmen were not merely surviving their freshmen years; they were thriving. A careful examination of the numbers revealed that the same students were incurring most of the infractions listed above.

Every teacher who has been in the classroom for more than three or four days discovers the 80/20 Rule: twenty percent of the students cause eighty percent of the problems. With our freshmen, that ratio was fairly accurate. Twenty percent of the students accounted for eighty percent of the F-List and were getting about eighty percent of the discipline referrals. The positive side of this ratio, however, indicates that a great many freshmen were transitioning smoothly into Goshen High School; joining sports, clubs, music, and drama programs; passing core academic and elective classes; and generally following the norms and protocols of the school. We did not want to lose sight of the fact that GHS was working for lots of the students, and we did not want to make changes that could significantly alter successful programs and initiatives. So we needed to make changes, but we wanted to be selective and target those students who were located in that somewhat nebulous gray area between *incorrigible* and *successful*. Our target students, therefore, became the "bubble kids," the kids that were almost successful and could be successful if they were provided with a little extra help and support.

Our First Steps

College Potential:

One program that was already in place and had starting paying dividends was the College Potential program. This initiative had been started by our guidance counselors in the 2000-2001 school year. College Potential (CP) identifies about 25 students at the end of their eighth grade year who, as the name implies, have potential to become college or university students but may need some extra support or encouragement to meet this goal.

The College Potential student profile states: "Students are academically capable of succeeding in college but may have some barriers that could prevent their future enrollment (lack of finances, first-generation college students, single parents, etc.). The eighth grade counselor selects students who are ready for Biology I and Algebra I as freshmen and who could benefit from exposure to college campuses."

The CP program groups students together for their math and science classes in both grades 9 and 10. During these two years, the class follows the regular curriculum and takes field trips to college campuses. Seniors who were in College Potential will be eligible for a college scholarship, usually $500, through the Dollars for Scholars program.

Comments from College Potential Students

"Never before had I thought about continuing my education after high school because my parents did not expect it. The College Potential program opened up many doors, ideas, and opportunities for me. It is because of College Potential that I will be attending Purdue.'
Jaime Munoz-Anaya, 2003 graduate and scholarship winner.

"The best part is getting the chance to see colleges before I have to make a decision." Brittney Dudeck, 2003 graduate.

"Being selected as a College Potential student was a privilege for me. I learned that grades and attitude are the two big things you need to succeed in high school."
Amber Koenig, 2003 graduate.

The results from the program have been very positive. We have had three graduating classes involved in College Potential. Of these students, 17% graduated with an Academic Honors diploma, Indiana's most rigorous diploma. Of these students, 17% graduated with an Academic Honors diploma, Indiana's most rigorous diploma. Another 45% graduated with the Core 40 diploma, which automatically qualifies them for entrance to our state universities. Half of the College Potential students enroll in a four-year college or university upon graduation, and an additional 25% enter two-year degree programs or the military services. These numbers are significantly higher than those of similar GHS students who did not participate in the College Potential program.

From a College Potential Teacher

Working with the College Potential program since its inception has been a very rewarding experience for me. The most enjoyable part has been the relationships that I have formed with the CP students. This has happened largely because I have had the same group of students for an entire year, and in some cases, two years. In our non-College Potential courses, students are shuffled at semester, so it is hard to establish the depth and quality of the relationships that I have established with the CP students over the years. It is my former CP students who stop in regularly just to say hello or touch base.

Not only have I enjoyed forming relationships with the students, but I have also enjoyed watching them form close friendships with each other. By the end of two years of having two classes together each year, there is quite a sense of camaraderie between the students. They have formed their own smaller learning community.

I strongly believe that the relationships between the students themselves and between the students and myself have allowed them to achieve higher academic success than they would have otherwise. An example of this is last year's chemistry class. Every student in that class earned an A or a B for both marking periods during the second semester. This cannot be said for any of the other regular chemistry courses. In addition to this, many of the CP students have gone on to take challenging upper-level science courses and have been very successful in them.

CHRIS WEAVER, College Potential Teacher

Freshman Academy:

The students that were academically above the College Potential (CP) students were already being very successful, and the CP program generally helped to pull a group of about 25 more freshmen a few rungs further up the academic ladder by setting high goals and extra support. This still left us with a group of freshmen that were sometimes struggling academically and did not qualify for extra support from either the special needs or the English as a New Language (ENL) programs. We came to this not terribly startling realization about the same time that we were holding the leadership meetings at the downtown Chamber of Commerce offices. (See Chapter One.)

Out of that time of intentional team building, the GHS administrators asked for and received a handful of volunteers who were willing to take the time to examine the "freshman problem" more closely and design a course of action. This initial planning group consisted of six teachers, two guidance counselors, an employee of the local Boys and Girls Club, our English as a New Language (ENL) academic advisor, our School Resource Officer, and an assistant principal. Three of the teachers were in their first few years of teaching; one was a reading specialist; and all were from the core academic courses of English, science, and math.

This planning group took a series of professional leave days during which they met at the home of the assistant principal for brainstorming and dreaming. They examined the data on the freshmen and soon became convinced that their small group could not solve all the freshmen problems, but they could make a difference in the academic performance by targeting specific students. Furthermore, this group believed it could positively impact the culture of Goshen High School and could significantly improve student performance on the ISTEP/GQE, the Indiana high-stakes standardized test, which is given in the fall of a student's tenth grade year. Out of this somewhat inexperienced and diverse group, Goshen High School's Freshman Academy was born in the spring of 2003.

We debated for some time about the scope of the Academy. We talked to and visited with some great educators at schools that were doing good things with programs that included all of the freshmen. Eventually, we decided we would pilot a program, keep data, and then decide whether the program should be changed, abandoned, or expanded. We kept coming back to one idea: while many of our freshmen were having difficulty, more were not. Therefore, our pilot Freshman Academy group consisted of 75 students whom we thought would benefit from a team approach and who needed extra time and support to make academic improvements. We decided that these students would take English 9, Algebra I, Biology I, and if they needed support in language arts or math—which most did—they would take Reading/Writing Lab and/or Math Readiness. These "double-up" classes would be taken for elective credit and would provide additional time on basic skills in the two areas that are assessed on our statewide high stakes test. Goshen High School is on a modified Block 8 Schedule (see Appendix), so the Academy students would take four or five of their classes with Academy teachers and the others with teachers outside the Academy in elective areas.

We had used "Double-Up" classes before we had Freshman Academy and had tracked data for several years in both the English and Math Departments. We had discovered that students who take Algebra I and along with Math Readiness improve at a significant rate. According to our Northwest Education Assessment (NWEA, also known as MAP) scores, our students who take Math Readiness and Algebra I, essentially doubling their time on math, will gain over a full year's growth in math in one semester. The same is true of our students who took English 9 and Reading/Writing Lab. In one semester, these students made well over a full year's growth in reading as based on the results of the NWEA test scores.

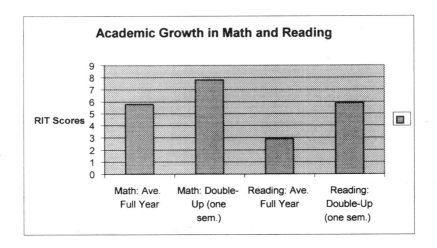

Values and Vision

Before we began the actual process of choosing students for Freshman Academy, we set values, vision, and goals. For this planning group, Core Values made the most sense as a place to start, so in April of 2003, we developed the following Core Values for the Freshman Academy program:

- Relationship Based: Teachers, counselors, administrators, and staff would intentionally work to create positive relationships with Freshman Academy students. This process would begin before school even started and continue after students had moved on from the Academy.
- Safe/Comfortable: Teachers would create comfortable learning environments where all students feel welcomed, wanted, and safe.
- High Expectations: Freshman Academy students would be held to the same high academic standards and essential learning as all other students.
- Involved/Connected to School: Freshman Academy students would be expected to form attachments to the school and become involved in Goshen High School outside of the classroom.

Those four values then led to the development of the vision for Freshman Academy:

Students:
- Will set individual goals that are realistic and positive
- Will have high expectations for personal performance and involvement
- Will accept responsibility for their own learning and growth
- Will value their school experience
- Will integrate and value their diverse backgrounds

Parents:
- Will be partners in the Freshman Academy
- Will be invited to participate in their child's success
- Will feel comfortable participating in Academy activities
- Will receive frequent communication
- Will receive accurate feedback on their child's academic success
- Will be part of the "village"

Staff:
- Will work in collaboration with each other in order to make the Academy successful
- Will develop and nurture teacher/student relationships
- Will celebrate success

Curriculum:

- Will be the regular Algebra, Biology, and English 9 Curriculum
- Will be based on state standards

Community:

- Will contribute to the success of the Academy and of the students

The Value of Positive Relationships

Often times we ask ourselves as educators what we can do to increase our students' performance and learning. We search and search for innovative lesson plans and engaging activities that will not only increase student learning but make them active participants in the classroom. While technology, better textbooks, audio-visual material, and hands-on labs all help, I feel the real key to student performance lies in the student/teacher relationship. What we have found out in Freshmen Academy is that students will perform and will raise the expectations for themselves when they feel that groups of people truly care about them and their well-being.

When the students feel that teachers care about them and that teachers are investing time into them, the students will try to reciprocate that effort. It is critical that we get to know our students and not to identify them by a letter grade. Students have a very good understanding that relationships work both ways, and if the teachers show that they care and respect students, they will try to perform to please that teacher. The Freshmen Academy program has allowed a group of teachers to cultivate relationships. Of course the idea of relationship building is neither new nor innovative, but often educators overlook the importance of relationships. The reasons for this are many: classes can be too large, students change schedules, and teachers are required to cover a vast amount of material in a short amount of time. All of these reasons decrease the amount of time to build relationships.

The Freshmen Academy program at Goshen High School has given me the opportunity to build positive relationships with my students. We have small class sizes, their schedules remain consistent, and we see them all year long. While I will never claim to be an expert in my field, I will say that I excel at building relationships with my students. Students, staff, and parents have told me that it was the relationship that I forged with the students that helped them more than anything I ever taught them in the classroom.
DAVID WILSON, Freshman Academy Teacher

Choosing the Pilot Group

The target group for Freshman Academy, for the most part, included the students at the bottom of the third quartile and the top of the fourth quartile. Our reasoning was simple: we could make the most difference with this group. Since many of our students were doing well, we dropped down the academic ladder and focused on the "bubble kids," those students right at or just below the cut score for passing the eighth grade standardized test.

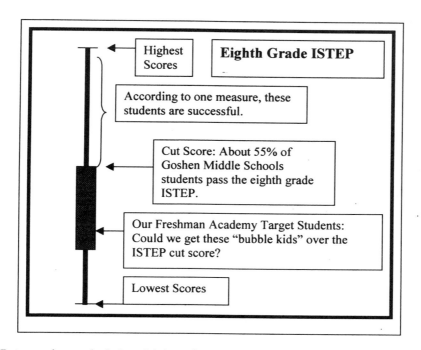

Between the matriculating eighth graders sent to us from Goshen Middle School and move-ins, we typically get between 400 and 450 ninth graders each year. For the purpose of identifying our Freshman Academy students, we started with the eighth grade ISTEP test scores. About 55% of the Goshen Middle School eighth graders pass their tests in English/Language Arts and Math, which left us with about 200 students below the cut score. As indicated in the demographic information in the first chapter, nearly one quarter of our students district-wide are ENL, so some of the eighth grade students below the cut score were in the English Language Learner pipeline and would eventually be integrated into general education classes. Other eighth students were in self-contained special needs classes and were thus removed from our target group.

We began working with the pilot group of 75 Freshman Academy students in the spring of 2003, while they were still in eighth grade. In the 2004-2005 school year, Freshman Academy was expanded to two teams, with 75 students and five teachers in each team. We currently have no plans to expand beyond these 150 students. With the help of the middle school eighth grade principal, guidance counselor, and teachers, we identified the target students based on ISTEP results, grades, attendance, and teacher recommendations. High school teachers, guidance counselors, and administrators met with the students to introduce them to the Freshman Academy program, and we fed them pizza and pop. Our first learning: feed them, and they will come.

We talked to these students about expectations at the high school, about the Graduation Qualifying Exam, about what we know about what successful students do and asked them to help us help them to be successful. Each student was sent home with a Plan for Success, which is copied below. This document summarizes the essence of the Freshman Academy, and each student and the student's parent or guardian were required to sign the Plan for Success in order to be included in Freshman Academy.

Each year the student meetings were followed by mailings home to parents or guardians, which invited the students and parents to an informational meeting to be held in the evening at Goshen High School. This May meeting was attended by about 20 of the 75 families from each Academy. We made an effort to celebrate with those who came to the meeting, rather than dwell on those that did not attend. Of the families that did attend, all signed the Plan for Success. The high school guidance counselors, who became our primary salespeople for the Freshman Academy program, contacted those families that did not attend the evening meeting. The counselors made individual appointments with students and parents, explained the program, and then scheduled students either into or out of the program.

In the first year, we had five families of the 75 originally identified who opted out of the Freshman Academy program. About the same percentage chose not to commit to Freshman Academy during the second and third years. Alternates from the original lists replaced these students. Other students were added as they moved into our district if they fit the profile for our target students. We made case-by-case decisions on these students with input from parents and the students themselves.

Building Relationships: Teachers Who Care

- Academy size limited to 75 students per team
- Multidisciplinary educational teams
- A mentor for every student
- Celebration times
- Additional time provided
- *Timely interventions*

A Plan for Success

I understand the importance of my first year of high school, and I want to do everything I can to make this year successful. Therefore, I agree to the following:

Attend each class every day possible: Since I am aware that a primary indicator of success in school is attendance, I will maintain an attendance rate of at least 95% and will have my parents/guardians hold me accountable for my attendance. When situations arise where I need to miss school, I will make sure my parents/guardians verify my absences. I will also ensure that I make up all assignments I missed during my absence.

Participate in school activities: Since I am aware that students who get involved in school activities tend to perform better in the classroom, at Goshen High School I will join and participate regularly in an extracurricular activity such as, but not limited to, the following: band, choir, orchestra, drama productions, any club, sport, or academic team each nine weeks.

Come to this summer's and next summer's activities: Because I want to transition smoothly into Goshen High School and because I want to do well on the ISTEP/GQE, I will come to activities planned for this summer and next summer.

Do my best in all my classes and am willing to focus on core academic courses: Since I know that the classes I take my freshman year of high school provide the building blocks for future classes and open up a wide range of future opportunities, I will focus on core academic classes for my freshman year. I know that the teachers and staff want me to succeed; however, I will be responsible for seeking extra help when I need it and will use resource time wisely and efficiently.

_____

Student Name (Print)

_____   Date _____

Student Signature

_____   Date _____

Parent Signature

Contact: Home Phone _____

                Work Phone _____

        Parent's email _____

Introducing students to GHS

We don't have this process perfected by any means, but we do try to help Freshman Academy students feel comfortable as they transition into high school. During the summer before school starts, we try to meet with Freshman Academy students in several ways. First, the Academy teachers, working in teams of two, contact each Freshman Academy student and spend several days making home visits. These visits are not long and do not reach every student, but the visits do serve to introduce the students to their soon-to-be teachers and begin to establish a tone for the year. Secondly, we invite through both mailings and by phone calls all Freshman Academy students to meet on a July evening. During that time, we do some group building exercises, we talk about the coming school year, answer questions, and eat. (Remember our first learning about food!) Finally, each Freshman Academy student is invited to Freshman Orientation, which takes place the day before school starts. This event is open to all freshmen. Transportation is provided both ways, and students get their final schedules, walk through a shortened schedule, meet all of their teachers, practice opening their lockers, have a snack so they can see the cafeteria, and pretend they aren't lost as they walk all over the school looking for their rooms.

Getting Involved:

Students who participate in activities do better in school.

- Summer Cookout
- Freshman Orientation
- 20 competitive athletic teams
- 20 interscholastic teams
- 8 competitive music groups
- 12+ student clubs
- Parties - study breakfast, holidays

Mentoring in Freshman Academy

Being a mentor of eight students in Freshmen Academy was possibly the most rewarding part of my experience. At the beginning of the year, each teacher selected students they would "watch over" throughout the year. I had only met with the students for one class period, so my selections were rather random. I ended up with eight: five girls (2- Caucasian, 3- Latina), three boys (all Latino). Four of these students I chose because they seemed very quiet and not to have many friends. Two seemed to have developed a defensiveness and hostility to persons in authority. Two seemed somewhat popular and outgoing.

One of the first steps I took as a new mentor was to introduce myself in that role to the students I had chosen. They all seemed to feel flattered that *I* had chosen *them*. I defined what I saw as my role as mentor—to keep track of their academic, social, and emotional progress. I told them that I would celebrate their successes and share in their journey through ninth grade.

Every week, I would check my students' grades. If they were doing well, I would be sure to give positive feedback at some point during that week. It was such a simple thing—as I am standing in the hallways before class with students entering my room, I would put my hand up for a high five "nice work in Bio" or I would simply lean in "up to a B in Health." If they were doing poorly, I would ask what was happening and encourage them to talk to the teacher and get into a resource room. It cost me nothing and made all the difference. These students realized that I was watching. They knew that I cared.

Mr. Garvin, the English 9 teacher in our Academy, and I decided to take our mentees to an arcade and amusement place. We covered the cost of admittance. Once there, we played miniature golf, laser tag, jousting, air hockey, and lots of video games. I admit that I elected to play air hockey and miniature golf, leaving Mr. Garvin to the laser tag and jousting, which he dominated. This activity did cost time and money, but the rewards were profound. Some of the students used this time to open up to me and share parts of themselves that they would have otherwise not. In the classroom, they became my champions and bragged about how much fun they had.

As the year moved on, I would send them cards, notes of inspiration, and even small gifts for celebrations or holidays. In return, I met many of their parents and was invited to a *quinceañera*.

Despite their differences, my mentees grew into students who felt accepted and successful. They were willing to take risks and make mistakes. They learned about accepting responsibility and dealing with others. Each of my mentees passed the ninth grade, most with high scores.

Feeling accepted and even important can be the difference between success and failure. I will continue to keep my eye on two of the students who seem to need more support as they move through tenth grade. I will always be a person each of the eight can come to share and feel safe, cared for, and welcome. I may even see them in my junior/senior writing class.

As the next group of freshmen arrives, and I select more mentees, my challenge and goal will be to continue to maintain old relationships while creating new one. I even see ways my previous mentees might be helpful in acclimating new freshmen.

JAIME SHREINER, Freshman Academy Teacher

During the School Year:

The special attention for Freshman Academy students does not stop during the school year. We make an effort to keep our program flexible and many of the items on the following list evolved as we met and adjusted to events or circumstances:

- **Friday Meetings**: Almost by accident, Freshman Academy personnel discovered that we needed to meet often to make sure we were communicating. The result was that we began to meet weekly before school from 7:30 to 8:00. During these times, we discuss upcoming activities, specific students, and try to be proactive with interventions. The Friday meetings involve the teachers, several guidance counselors, and several assistant principals.

- **Keep the focus on academic success**: It did not take us long to figure out that we cannot solve all our students' problems. Many of our Academy students have issues that have gotten in the way of their academic success. Sometimes we can "fix" these problems, but often we can't. We don't ignore problems outside of academics, but we keep our focus on those things that we can control. We teach coping strategies and basic study skills. Many of our Freshman Academy students don't know how to "do school." We intentionally teach them these skills. In a variety of ways, we say to them, "This is what good students do. This is how you can be successful in school." Then we try to show them that they too can be great students.

- **Email**: Our emails have become extremely important in tracking students. Even with weekly meetings, communication between FA staff is difficult. Another practice that has evolved is using the group email. The "reply all" button is useful to keep everyone updated. A word of warning: the tone and content of emails are, at times, easy to misunderstand. We have had to work on being exact and using the correct tone in emails.

- **Parties and Activities**: Part of our vision is that we celebrate success. These celebrations have taken many forms. We have had holiday parties and ice cream treats. We provided a hot breakfast before final exams, and we celebrated the end of the school year and the progress we made. Students often mention these celebrations as one of the positives of Freshman Academy in their end of the year evaluations. Their importance should not be underestimated.

- **School Resource Officer**: We have a Goshen city police officer assigned to the school, and we have used him to follow up on missing students. Our unofficial guideline is that as soon as a student is absent for more than two days without notification to the school, we follow up with phone calls. If we can't reach the student, we send out our SRO to make contact or leave a note. Officer Johnson, known at school as OJ, will also go and pick up students who missed the bus or who have no way to school. It is good public relations for both the school and the police department.

- **Mentor/Mentees**: One of the initiatives that we are still trying to figure out is matching each FA student to a mentor. The first year, we did this within the FA program. Each FA teacher, all four guidance counselors, and the assistant principal took on 5-10 FA students to mentor or give special attention to during the school year. The second year, we expanded this to all administrators and even to central office administrators. The results have been mixed. For students who have mentors that are actively involved with the students, the benefits have been remarkable. Active mentors monitor student progress, provide support, and get immediate interventions when needed. Some students, however, had little contact with their mentors, and this caused some hard feelings and resentment. The concept is excellent, and one of our goals for the coming year is to bring more structure to this initiative. It has potential to become a major piece of the FA experience.

- **Professional Leave**: During the school year, we take intentional time out to reflect. These days have taken two forms so far. The first is a full day for all staff involved in FA to reflect on progress. The first half of the day is spent looking at what is going well and what needs improvement. Then a plan is developed and put into place for programmatic changes. In the afternoon, we divide by teams and talk about specific students and develop individual plans and interventions for students. The second type of professional leave we call Intervention Days. On these days, the Academy teachers meet with about 20 students individually and talk to them about the positives they have seen with the students and about their concerns. These meetings take between 15 minutes and a half hour for each student. Together, the student and the teachers develop short-term goals and a plan of action for both the student and the teachers in order to help the student become more successful academically. They establish timelines and follow up with the student, sometimes on the next Intervention Day and sometimes more often. The teachers and students have found these days to be profound and even life-changing experiences. We will continue to use these days as an important part of the FA experience.

Simple Interventions Can Make a Big Difference

An Academy teacher discovered that she had 60 students with a D+ or below in the math support class. She sent home a note and a current grade report to each home.

The result: Less than two weeks later, only 31 students had a D+ or below. Sure, it's still a problem, but a better one than before!

I feel fortunate that I am a Freshman Academy teacher and have been involved with the program since the beginning planning sessions. Intervention Days have evolved over time; they began during the second semester of the 2004-2005 school year in the second year of the FA program. Despite needing to write sub plans and miss classroom time, as a Freshman Academy team we have found these Intervention Days to be invaluable.

As a team we prioritize which students we need to see. We try to see students that aren't achieving success at that time, students we feel have potential to get things turned around, and students that have slipped academically or behaviorally. When we call a student into the conference room, we reassure them they aren't in trouble and try to set them at ease. We begin with the positives, what the student is doing well. Following that, we bring up whatever issue(s) that are of concern. We ask students for their input: Do they agree that the issue is a problem? What do they think is causing it? What suggestions do they have for improvement? Then we have a group discussion and make a plan. We document the strategies to be tried, people that will be involved, and a target date for a follow-up on an intervention form. The student signs the form.

Our experience has been that some students really open up about their situations and feelings; other don't share as much personally, but they still indicate that they are impressed their teachers care so much. When we saw students for the second and third times, the meetings became smoother and more productive. It was great to see the students' reactions, especially for the many that experienced improvement or success.

I'm very excited about the coming school year because we have already chosen the Intervention Day dates. Each team member will do some pre-intervention work to bring to the conferences. As we become more structured and experienced, we will be able to increase the number of students we work with and the quality of interventions.
CINDY SWIHART, Freshman Academy Teacher

The bumps in the road:

We have had many minor problems with Freshman Academy. For example, issues sometimes arise over how to deal with an especially difficult student, who is going to provide an intervention, or philosophical differences about grading or discipline. Most of these "bumps" have been handled routinely as part of the Friday meeting time or during a professional leave day. One issue that we did not handle as routinely was the expansion process during the second year of FA. During the pilot year of 2003-2004, the five teachers that worked with FA were included very early into the planning process. Several were involved from the very beginning as part of the group that met to discuss the "freshman problem." This group was given the difficult task of turning an idea into reality, but they also had considerable freedom to make changes and adjustments and through the process began to "own" Freshman Academy. They were and are an unusual mix of teachers and in many ways have very different teaching approaches. They also have the unique ability to disagree with each other, but still recognize the gifts the others bring to the table. They allow each other a great deal of freedom and grace.

In the fall of 2004, we added five more teachers to this mix, each with a slightly different degree of commitment to and belief in the Freshman Academy program. We also added a second assistant principal. All five of the newly added FA teachers are excellent teachers, and the new assistant principal is outstanding. In hindsight, however, we did not allow enough time or space for the "new" Academy to develop its own culture and way of operating. The established Academy teachers had developed through trial and error a way of working that fit their personalities and styles. The newly added teachers, without the same background and experience, struggled with how to fit into the established culture and wondered if they should even try to do so. The result was that the new and larger group had difficulty developing cohesion and unity of process. We seemed to have agreement on the purpose of the Academy and certainly a commitment to the students, but the two groups did not meld well.

Soon into the school year, we came to a somewhat uneasy agreement to have the teams work semi-independently, and this seemed to help. This division, which seems a bit counterintuitive, actually contributed to a strong second semester in the spring of 2005. The teams each tried different interventions and were able to share these with the other. Each team was able to operate in ways that felt most comfortable, and the results have been positive enough that we are planning to keep the teams somewhat autonomous in the coming school year. We have had one teacher opt out of the Academy for next year, and a second teacher moved with her husband out of the Goshen area, so the new team will again be "new" this coming year.

The Results

There are, of course, many ways to measure a success or failure of the program. By most measures, the Freshman Academy program has been successful. At the end of both school years, we asked students to evaluate their experience. The results of these surveys have been overwhelmingly positive, especially about the FA teachers and the effort and concern they have for their students. On a scale of 1 to 5, with 5 being the most positive score, our FA students responses to 10 survey questions average 4.2. Remember that these are freshman who in the past have not had the most positive experience in school!

Comments from Two FA Students, May 2005

"I was so excited to get my progress report last week. I had great grades. I was doing poorly the first semester because I wasn't focused. But now I'm cutting back on the things that held me back (like video games) and really starting to focus."

"My spring break I was grounded for my grades. And I'm pretty excited about the coming of the last day of school. The Academy really helped me set my priorities straight, especially Mr. Wilson's lectures. And it also helps that all the teachers in the Academy are funny, helpful, and cheery."

We also have some positive objective results as well. With the current emphasis on standardized testing, we know that a program like Freshman Academy must make a significant difference on our scores. As the chart below indicates, our Freshman Academy students did make progress. In grade 8, about 20% of these students passed the state standardized test in English/Language Arts, and about 20% passed the math portion. At the beginning of their sophomore year, 42% passed the English/ Language Arts test and 62% passed the math portion. Our English scores we believe to be slightly lower because of the large number of ENL students (about 25%) in the Academy, but we are working to improve these numbers.

The other charts below provide other indicators of academic growth:

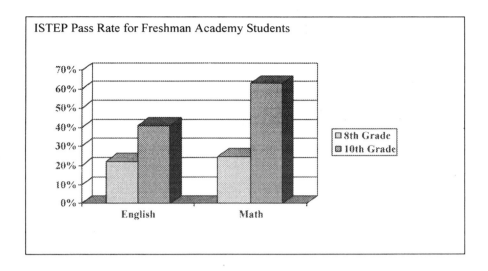

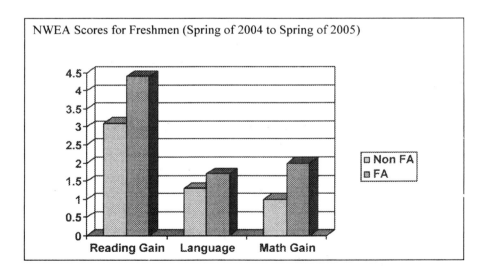

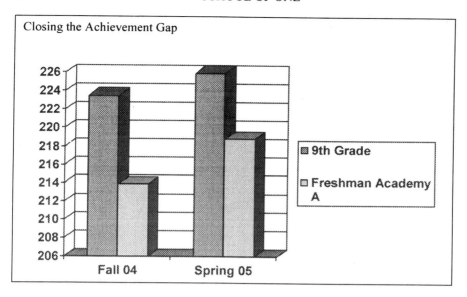

Closing the Achievement Gap

From the first year of Freshman Academy, we also have the following data:

- Credits earned: FA students earned an average of 12.33 credits. Most freshmen earn a total of 13 or 14 credits, depending on whether they took Physical Education, which counts as only 0.5 credits per semester, so we were very pleased with this total.

- GPA: The average Grade Point Average for FA students was 2.134.

- Attendance: The average FA student missed a little less than 8 days of school during the 2003-2004 school year. Several students received a disproportionate number of these absences, so the average is a bit skewed.

- Discipline: The average FA student received 3.5 discipline referrals during the 2003-2004 school year, but over half of the FA students received no discipline referrals at all.

- Preliminary data on the first year FA students indicate that most of these students had a successful sophomore year. We will continue to track their progress as they complete their high school careers.

Our Next Steps with Freshman Academy:

In the coming school year (2005-2006), we will continue with the two Academy model. Two of the assistant principals will coordinate the efforts of the Academy teams. As stated earlier, one team is in a rebuilding process because two of the five teachers left at the end of the school year. This coming year, we will spend more time providing time for the new teachers to learn the history and vision of the academy. The teams will continue to function somewhat independently, but we will continue to get together throughout the school year to compare what is and is not working.

At the end of the 2005-2006 school year, the FA teachers set the following goals for the coming year:

- Provide more timely interventions. How do we identify students that need help more quickly and get them what they need in a timely manner? How do we connect FA students to community services when they need assistance which our teachers and school are unable to provide? We will be working in cooperation with the guidance department and SRT teachers to put some of these interventions into place.

- Work on the student involvement piece. We need to find ways to follow up and hold students accountable for being involved at GHS. We know that students who are involved do better in school. How do we make sure students really do get connected to our high school?

- Find structures and guidelines for the mentor/mentee relationship that will ensure that all students have a positive experience from this relationship.

None of these are easy tasks, but they will provide the focus for our efforts in this coming year.

Opportunity Knocks: One More Attempt to Keep Students on Track

In the spring of 2004, we were feeling good about the programs and initiatives we had in place for many of our students. The students at the top of the academic ladder have always been successful. The College Potential program was working with kids that generally have good academic success and limited behavioral issues but could use some extra support to get them thinking about future academic careers. The Freshman Academy program was finishing its first year with positive results. The ENL students have special programs and initiatives designed to meet many of their academic needs, and the special needs students also have programs and teachers designed to support their needs. If a student didn't fit into any of these programs and was still unsuccessful, we also have Merit Learning Center, our alternative school, that gives a placement to freshmen who struggle in the traditional high school setting.

The problem was that freshmen that left for Merit were failing miserably. Merit is a great program and has been wonderful for many students, but the most successful Merit students are upperclassmen. Perhaps freshmen are too immature for the Merit requirements, perhaps they cannot see the light at the end of the high school tunnel, perhaps even the small setting of Merit is too big, or perhaps some other reason or a combination of all these caused problems for our freshman Merit students. Whatever the reason, we discovered that when all else had failed and our only option was Merit, almost universally, freshman at Merit were not passing classes, were not attending regularly, and were dropping out as soon as they legally could. Out of this realization, Opportunity Knocks was born.

This program is the smallest of the freshman initiatives. It is designed for 15-20 of our most at-risk freshman and is essentially a small alternative school, based in one classroom. Opportunity Knocks was originally going to be housed in the Goshen Sash and Door building—thus the unusual name—which is just off campus from GHS. Last minute changes moved the self-contained classroom into Goshen High School itself. The premise is that these at-risk freshmen would spend at least half their day with one teacher who would get to know them very, very well. This teacher would provide some off-line work, but most of the curriculum would be delivered through PLATO, an individualized computer based curriculum resource. The course work in Opportunity Knocks consists of English 9, Algebra I, and Job Skills, and the goal is to give these students options.

On the following pages is a letter sent to parents that explains the options for Opportunity Knocks (OK) students:

Goshen High School

401 Lincolnway East
Goshen, IN 46526

May 5, 2005

Dear Parents:

Your student will soon leave Goshen Middle School and enter Goshen High School. This is an exciting, but sometimes frightening, transition. We want to do everything we can to make the transition smooth and successful.

We have been in close contact with your student's middle school guidance counselor and principal. For a variety of reasons, they and we are recommending that your student participate in our Opportunity Knocks Program.

This program offers a very flexible approach to your student's education. We want your student to experience academic success, and we are prepared to provide an individual student plan for you child.

The heart of Opportunity Knocks is a self-contained class that will meet on campus in a self-contained classroom at Goshen High School. Your student will attend the Opportunity Knocks classroom from about 8:20 a.m. to 11:30 a.m. In that classroom, your student will study English, Algebra, and Job Skills. Your child will have one teacher who will develop a strong relationship with and provide support for your child. This teacher will also help your student prepare for the Graduation Qualifying Exam which will be taken in the fall of 2006.

After your student finishes Opportunity Knocks at 11:30, you and your student will have a variety of options. If you look at the attached sheet, you can see what some of these options might be.

We are very excited about the possibilities for your student, and we will do everything we can to help your student transition smoothly and successfully to high school and/or to work.

If you have questions, please contact your student's guidance counselor or me. We can be reached at 533-8651.

Sincerely,

Phil Lederach

Opportunity Knocks: Options

Every OK student will take three courses at the OK classroom. These classes are English, Algebra, and Job Skills. Our goal is to get the student ready for the ISTEP/GQE and/or to prepare the student for a successful working experience.

After spending the morning in the OK classroom, if the student and parent are supportive and interested, the student will take afternoon classes at GHS. These classes will be hand picked by the student, parent, and guidance counselor. They should pick courses that are interesting to the student and in which the student can be successful. The student could pick up to four courses.

If the student, parent, and counselor anticipate difficulties for the student in these afternoon classes, then the parents could opt for a reduced schedule. The reduced schedule might include three, two, one, or zero electives. If a student has a reduced schedule, he or she will be encouraged to find a job placement. If the student cannot find a placement, he or she will go home. WARNING: Transportation will be an issue for students on a reduced schedule, and students must earn nine (9) credits in order to advance to grade 10. The OK program can help a student earn three to five credits in a year. Therefore, a student must earn more credits beyond the OK program in order to advance to grade 10.

Possible Schedules:

Option A:

8:20-11:30 OK for English, Algebra, and Job Skills
11:30-3:15 Periods 4-7 at GHS for four high interest classes
Option B:

8:20-11:30 OK for English, Algebra, and Job Skills
11:30-3:15 Zero to Three high interest classes, plus a job placement of some kind.
(If a student leaves before 3:15, transportation must be provided.)
Option C:

8:20-11:30 OK for English, Algebra, and Job Skills
11:30: Student returns home. (WARNING: Student may not earn enough credits.)
(Transportation must be provided.)

Options at the end of the year:
1. Transition to full time at GHS.
2. Transition to part time GHS/Part time Merit Learning Center
3. Transition to full time Merit Learning Center/Job Placement
4. Transition to full time Merit Learning Center
5. Transition to full time in work force/GED program
6. Transition to full time in work force/Withdraw from school

Possible Schedules

Option A:

- 8:10   The bus drops off the student at GHS, or the student walks or drives to school
- 8:20-11:15   Class at the OK classroom (Students will take English, Algebra, and Job Skills.)
- 11:30-3:15   Periods 4-7 at GHS for four high interest classes

Option B:

- 8:10   The bus drops off the student at GHS, or the student walks or drives to school
- 8:20-11:15   Class at the OK classroom. (Students will take English 9, Algebra, and Job Skills.)
- 11:30-?   A student will take one, two, or three of these classes:
  Fourth Hour: 11:31-1:37 Tuesday/Thursday (Monday shorter)
  Fifth Hour: 11:31-1:37 Wednesday/Friday (Monday shorter)
  Sixth Hour: 1:44-3:15 Tuesday/Thursday (Monday shorter)
  Seventh Hour: 1:44-3:15 Wednesday/Friday (Monday shorter)

Option C:

- 8:10   The bus drops off the student at GHS, or the student walks or drives to school.
- 8:20-11:15   Class at the OK classroom. (Students will take English 9, Algebra, and Job Skills.)
- 11:20   The student goes to a job placement (if he or she has one), or the student goes home if there is no job placement.

After getting school board approval and writing the state required waivers, we hired an outstanding young social studies teacher, Ms. Jenny Clark, to begin this program. She also had the assistance of an aide during the morning hours when OK is operational. It was a rocky beginning for Ms. Clark because furniture and computers did not arrive on time, but before long, she was up and running and had an extremely successful first year.

Students can enter the OK program at any time during the school year, so their work, by necessity, is individualized. With the help of the English and Math departments, Ms. Clark set up a standards-based curriculum for English 9 and Algebra I. She used the curriculum from the Job Skills class that is taught in both the School-to-Work program and in the special needs department. She soon discovered that most of the OK students had major gaps in their math and English basics. Fortunately, the PLATO program provides interventions for students, and her students worked through the remediation if it was needed and simultaneously began on course work.

From the Teacher's Perspective

When I chose teaching as my career path and social studies as my content area, I pictured myself in a U.S. History or Government class. While I still get to fit social studies into my day, my most rewarding experiences come from a group of students who are often seen as less desirable. Patience, patience, and more patience has been my saving grace while working with the Opportunity Knocks program. These students come to me everyday with a variety of needs, from academic to social to behavioral. Yet, even through the challenges, I've seen first hand how the flexibility of this program results in students improving their attendance, finding academic success, and being proud of their accomplishments.

Now that Opportunity Knocks is in its second year, I see students from last year and am so proud of what they continue to do. Some remain at Goshen High School, while others are now at the Merit Learning Center. Some are true sophomores and are well adjusted to high school life, while others continue to struggle. No matter their current status, I look forward to following these students.

JENNY CLARK--Opportunity Knocks teacher

As to be expected from these extremely at-risk students, the Opportunity Knocks kids battled Ms. Clark, but she was able to persevere and eventually built her room into a community of learners. By the end of the year, her walls were covered with certificates recognizing the academic achievement of her students, and her discipline structure also helped students make significant behavioral progress as well. Ms. Clark kept the OK students with her for Student

Resource Time, and she tracked her students' progress in classes outside of the OK program (if they took other classes) and provided help and structure for her students in these elective classes.

Not all of the OK students were successful, but we do have some amazing success stories. Ms. Clark tracked individual student progress on graphs like the one shown below.

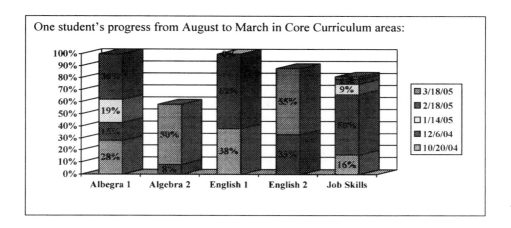

At first glance this data may not look impressive, but to those of us know these students personally and know the past success rates with students like these, we are more than impressed. We are convinced that these students would have had little or no success given their options before Opportunity Knocks. In the first year of the Opportunity Knocks, we had 23 students enrolled. Four students transferred into other schools during the school year, and two received court-ordered placements. The average enrollment was fifteen, but because of poor attendance habits—which we were unsuccessful in changing—the average daily attendance in the classroom was closer to thirteen.

Fourteen students spent most of their year in the Opportunity Knocks program, and we have based our numbers on these students. These students earned 51 credits inside the OK program and 59 credits outside the program, either in regular education classes or through school-to-work credits that involved a job placement. This averages out to 7.8 credits per student. Of course most GHS freshmen earn 13 or 14 credits, but this result is significantly better than we were getting in the past when freshmen students left GHS in order to enroll in Merit Learning Center.

Furthermore, all fourteen students are enrolled to come back next year, either to GHS or to Merit Learning Center, and they now have had some success and understanding of what they need to do in order to make it in high school. Those who did not experience academic success at least have had one more year in school. They have had a positive relationship with a teacher who truly cares for them. They have done some work on their English and math skills and have thought about what will help them be successful workers. We will mourn if they choose to drop out of school, but we do know that we have done as much as we reasonably can to assist them and prepare them for life outside of school.

Summary

We are on a journey. We don't know exactly what our freshman initiatives will look like in the future. We suspect for the next few years that the combination of high expectations for all freshman, SRT, honors classes, College Potential, Freshman Academy, Opportunity Knocks, ENL classes and programs, and Special Needs classes and programs will provide the framework for what we do. These all may change or disappear as the needs of our students change. They all certainly will evolve.

We do not have all the answers. We are, however, convinced that we are asking many of the right questions about our freshmen: What is the right thing to do? How can we help more kids? How can we do this better? The questions are the constant. In the coming years, without a doubt, the answers will change. Our goal is to provide the flexibility required to meet the ever-changing needs of our students, especially of those sometimes exasperating but often very lovable freshmen. We know that if we can somehow "get them" when they are freshman, we have a very good chance of shaking their hands, patting their backs, and handing them diplomas a few years down the road.

Chapter 8

With the changing population, particularly in the area of students new to the United States, the Goshen staff knew that we had to be better informed in how we work with students of poverty. As a school district, we have some schools above 70 percent poverty students and the high school comes in the lowest with nearly 40 percent of the students on free or reduced lunch. The impetus behind the "School of One" comes from what we learned about the unique culture of poverty from studying the works of Ruby Payne. While Goshen High School has not lead the way in this study, the school corporation has invested time and resources into understanding this characteristic of our students. All urban schools must become versed on how these families function in their communities and in our schools.

Learning How Our Students View Life

BARRY YOUNGHANS, ASSISTANT SUPERINTENDENT

When I returned to Goshen Community Schools after a four year absence, there had been significant changes in the demographics of our school district. Most noticeable were the increases in English Language Learners and minorities. However, Goshen Schools also had an increasing number of students from poverty. While such changes certainly are not negative, they provide additional challenges to classroom teachers and the school system. The changing demographic factors, combined with the push for increased accountability, forced Goshen Schools to explore ways to improve instructional practices and student achievement.

I became aware of Ruby Payne's *Framework for Understanding Poverty* during the early 1990's. I realized it was "good stuff" but did not fully comprehend the possibilities it held for us.

One principal in our corporation saw its promise; Don Jantzi, principal at Chamberlain Elementary, really explored Dr. Payne's writings and her teaching methodology. Don saw this as crucial to his school's success because he had the highest poverty rate in the district.

While Mr. Jantzi was incorporating Ruby Payne into the culture at Chamberlain, I was an assistant principal at Goshen Middle School. I witnessed first hand some of the results of the Chamberlain staff's work. I saw the improvement in their ISTEP scores and their student's behavior. Payne's text held many potential benefits for the students and outstanding methodology for the teaching staff.

In the fall of 2001, I was named principal of Chandler Elementary. The staff at Chandler was also open to change and looking for ways to improve student achievement. Several teachers had already been exposed to Ruby Payne workshops, and as we explored possible routes to school improvement it became clear that working on specific strategies for children of poverty might be an option. We examined our demographics and we were approaching 50% free and reduced lunch status. We decided to make Ruby Payne one of our key components to school improvement. It cannot be overstated that this was a school decision not simply a mandate from the principal.

Early Childhood Education

Imagine you are a high school student tearing construction paper into tiny pieces to glue onto another piece of paper to make a picture. Imagine playing Freeze Tag or Duck, Duck, Goose during a high school class.

These are several of the "hands-on" activities that students in Early Childhood Education (ECE) assist with during class. The course focuses on all aspects of growth in very young children: cognitive, social, emotional, and physical. Students realize immediately the importance of a caregiver's consistent involvement with children. Students research activities that focus on the curricular topics we study, and then create developmentally appropriate activities for specific age groups.

The ECE program has its own kitchen to prepare healthy snacks for children and learn methods of food preparation appropriate to different ages. The students visit the public library to watch how professional storytellers relate to children and then select books to practice storytelling skills. Related to the classroom, students create science, math, and large motor skill activities for specific age groups and then all the students participate in that activity and evaluate the appropriateness for the age of the child.

When students have successfully completed Early Childhood Education, they may continue with the program by working in elementary classrooms, provide daycare for preschool or older children, or work in the Goshen Community Schools Child Care Center located in the high school building. The involvement with children and staff in a "real" classroom reinforces the information students learn in the ECE classroom. Students may decide to experience different age groups each semester or remain in the same classroom.

-JANE BROOKMYER—FACS teacher

The first step in our process was to send eight staff members to four different half-day training periods. I would call these trainings overviews that helped create additional awareness of Payne's methods. Two of our staff eventually became certified Ruby Payne trainers. One split his duties as a kindergarten teacher and a staff development facilitator, or coach. Beginning in the fall of 2002 and continuing on throughout that school year, all of our staff development focused on Ruby Payne. We began to turn theory into practice.

In addition to leading staff development, our coach also had several hours a week of direct student contact. Again, as a school we made a decision to place the coach in the position most likely to have a positive effect on ISTEP test. Since our tests were being administered in the fall of 3rd grade, the decision was made to place the coach in the second grade classes. During his student contact time, the coach utilized direct instruction to teach various skills such as test taking, improving communication and the use of mental models.

The increase in poverty levels of our students led us to explore how we could positively impact their education. However, as Goshen Community Schools travels down the path of school improvement, it is clear that Ruby Payne strategies will positively impact *all* students. In the years following 2002, each elementary school in our district has incorporated its own coach in a format that works for the specific school. In addition, the middle school has just completed training four trainers from their teaching staff.

G-JOBS in Action

In August of 2004, Goshen High School received a $9,000 grant from the Verizon Foundation to launch the Goshen Job Opportunities and Basic Skills (G-JOBS) program. The program was founded with the objective of helping Goshen High School's at-risk and special needs students obtain hands-on workplace training and eventual job placement.

The Special Needs Department established an unpaid work environment in Direct Service classes. Students completed landscaping projects planned and completed by the Job Skills classes. These projects were supported through community donations and small gardening grants. Throughout the process, students learned the skill of working directly under a supervisor in the form of various "foremen" randomly chosen from the class. The landscaping projects created a great sense of ownership and pride for the students. These work experiences were then bridged with the workforce development grant from Verizon in order to transition students into paid positions within the community.

The grant money allowed a Special Needs Job Skills teacher to be released from teaching in the afternoons in order to place students in jobs within the community. This also teacher administers work interest inventories and vocational aptitude assessments with the students to develop the most successful placements possible. Once students are placed in jobs, the teacher periodically checks in with the employers and the students to ensure the placement runs smoothly. The students not only receive pay for their work placements, they also earn high school credits based on number of hours worked.

At the beginning of the school year one special needs student decided he was ready to quit. He had not passed the Graduation Qualifying Exam and he saw no point in staying in school. He was the first student placed through the G-JOBS program. His schedule was changed so that he attended classes in the morning and then went to work in the afternoon with a local employer. His attendance improved along with his attitude toward school. Not only was he earning a steady paycheck and learning job skills, he was also earning credits towards graduation. At the end of the school year, he was offered fulltime employment for the summer, which he accepted. His employer stated that the goal was to train the student in various areas of

the business so that when he finished high school he would have a fulltime position with benefits available to him immediately if he wanted it. This student could have fallen through the cracks and been a casualty of the traditional education system if not for the G-JOBS program. The core belief behind the development of this program at Goshen High School is to offer an education beyond the traditional classroom in order to reach more students.
-JEN KALB

The benefits we learn from Ruby Payne will ultimately manifest themselves at Goshen High School. We will all have a common language for discussing students in poverty. Ruby Payne's methodology helps us create Goshen High School's ideal, the "School of One," through the emphasis placed on creating and maintaining meaningful relationships. We can build those relationships by understanding the specific educational, emotional, and social needs of kids from poverty.

Goshen schools certainly utilize Ruby Payne's methods on several levels. Each school is using it to answer one of the guiding questions of the learning model: "What will we do if students don't understand the essential skills?" It is one more tool in the teacher tool box to create an environment where all kids learn.

Chapter 9

In educating the entire child, a school must focus on academic challenges, but research shows that engaging students in extracurricular activities will also raise the success quotient for students. This chapter discusses the role of athletics and using the learning model within this department to make decisions.

Goshen High School Athletic Department and the Learning Model

LARRY KISSINGER, ATHLETIC DIRECTOR

Coaches have been using the learning model for ages. They identify what student-athletes need to know, practice it, assess it, and then keep trying to improve areas of weakness. With the help of professional development opportunities and from the history of coaching, the GHS athletic department identifies what students need to know for each specific sport. It could be argued that our academic "learning model" is what good athletic coaches have been doing for years. However, most of our coaches do not record what they want their student-athletes to learn, and are not aware that they are using a "learning model" at all.

Continuous training of staff is an essential aspect of the learning model. We have implemented a seasonal head coaches' meeting, a seasonal all coaches' meeting, and three all head coaches' meetings in an attempt to address athletic department concerns, give updates in technology, and promote the mission, vision, and value statements. Like in the classroom, our coaches are expected to keep current with teaching strategies. Goshen Community Schools requires all coaches to pass a certified coaching course, a standard that is more stringent than the requirements of the governing body of Indiana high school athletics (IHSAA). The Goshen High School athletic department encourages continued professional development by budgeting $10,000 per year toward professional development of head coaches and their staffs.

In the learning model the first step is to identify what needs to be learned. The GHS athletic department existed for decades without a mission statement, vision statements, or value statements. Recently, over a two-and-a-half-year period, the head coaches developed these pillars of who we are.

One of the vision statements is focused on "encouraging student-athletes to participate in multiple sports." Setting up summer schedules and off-season workouts are obvious areas that we have attempted to adjust to promote multi-sport participation. Our girls' basketball and volleyball coaches have begun running their youth camps in cooperation to promote participation in both sports. However, this has been more of an attitudinal change than a procedural change. In the recruiting process, student-athletes should see the difference. All coaches, when talking with student-athletes, should embrace the vision statements created by our head coaches.

All school years are different, but athletic support of academic excellence is one of the areas that can be critical for schools. The athletic department issues awards sponsored through local Kiwanis Clubs for maintaining a B or above grade point average. Each season is culminated with an awards ceremony night for all sports. At the last awards night, 63 percent of the athletes earned recognition for having a 3.0 grade point or higher. This is the highest percentage we have ever attained. This also supports the contentions of the Schlecty Center that engagement in school activities is another key factor in the success of students.

Coaches are also in an enviable position to help motivate student-athletes to perform better in the classroom. As a form of academic intervention, all head coaches receive copies of progress reports and report cards on student-athletes who earn a "D" or "F" in any class. This is done whether the student-athlete is currently in season or not. Coaches are expected to contact these student-athletes and help them pursue assistance. Coaches who also teach at Goshen High School can access grades, which are updated and sent out to the staff weekly. Several coaches have "study tables" for student athletes who struggle academically. However, several head coaches are not teachers at GHS, and therefore do not have access to weekly grades. The director of technology and I are working to remedy this problem in the coming years.

Currently, academic eligibility is determined every quarter. Many student-athletes participate while on failing status due to this setup. The next step is to investigate the concept of determining eligibility on a weekly basis to continue the emphasis on the importance of academics.

Chapter 10

While visiting Brazosport Schools, in Texas, one of the commitments the administration there made was to providing data to teachers for decision-making purposes. While these schools seemed almost uncomfortably focused on raising tests scores, their use of data allowed them to make instructional decisions that assisted students with their learning. When we were awarded a smaller learning community planning grant, the study committee recommended that we designate a data person to compile and distribute data to administration and staff. When we were received the regular Smaller Learning Community grant, the first move was to designate a teacher as our new data person. Our data person is also a doctoral student at Indiana University. Her pursuit of educational excellence coupled with her work ethic provides our school with constantly updated information including weekly progress of students. Her job also has her helping teachers get the information they need.

Using Data to Assist with Classroom Instruction and School Decision Making

SHELLY WILFONG, DATA SPECIALIST AND SOCIAL STUDIES

Teachers want to see simple, bottom-line data about the students in their own classrooms. Data can provide some of the answers to the following questions:

1. Are students learning?
2. What are students learning?
3. Are there particular areas or topics that students are struggling with?
4. Is the rate of growth above or below average?
5. If there are enough students, how are the subgroups performing?

When I tell people that I am a data person for my school, they usually give me a strange look. I teach social studies rather than math, which makes me a unique data person since most of the other data people I run into are either math teachers or administrators. However, I believe that my "non-math, not an administrator" background gives me an advantage.

Math teachers are usually too good at manipulating data. My non-math background allows me to make sure that teachers can easily understand data, and to be useful, data must be made simple. Teachers want to know which students are learning which skills. Keep it simple. (By the way, I love math teachers!)

Because I am a classroom teacher and not an administrator, my role is non-evaluative. Teachers can come to me with questions and concerns and not worry about it showing up on their next evaluation. This does make the position a little more difficult because the data portion of the job could easily be full time by itself. But I also teach the equivalent of four of six assigned teaching periods: three United States Government classes and one SRT class. The full time teaching load is six classes.

When creating or continuing a data program there are a few key ideas regarding the collection and presentation of data. All data should be:

Simple, regardless of how complex it seems at first. With limited resources it is important not to rely on expensive equipment or materials in order to collect most data. Teachers need to be able to use "Drive-Thru Data" as well as the expensive stuff. A nutritionist may disapprove of food from a "drive-thru," but sometimes convenience is a necessity. While professional surveys serve an important purpose, the results can take several months.

Quick, cheap, and easy to collect. There are a large number of data instruments that are helpful for teachers, but there is usually a cost associated with them. Most schools are not in a situation that they can ignore these costs. The key is to develop a system so that data is easy to compile with standard software such as Excel so that it can be manipulated.

Professionally safe for the teacher to collect. Teachers need systems to collect and analyze data quickly. With extensive standards, the prevailing feeling as that there is too much material to cover in the classroom and not enough time. Data collection during class time needs to be something that takes such little time that it does not take away from learning the content.

In addition, teachers need to feel that the data they collect will be used in a positive way. For some teachers, presenting data from their own classrooms can be very intimidating. Teachers are more willing to collect and present data as they become more confident and see colleagues sharing successes and failures.

Widely varied. The first data that comes to mind for teachers is usually test results, but there are many more types of useful data. With most student information systems, tracking grades and attendance can be done rather easily. It is important to remember that data can be collected regarding student behavior, but also can be compiled on areas such as teaching strategies.

Data can be collected in a variety of ways. When possible, it is nice to have colleagues observe each other, but this is not always possible due to conflicting schedules or the busy nature of teaching. Videotaping can be a good replacement.

Made a part of the classroom. Students need to understand how data affects them. If they can take ownership in the data collection and analysis portion then they can understand their own learning better. In some cases, depending on the subject area, it could even be integrated into the curriculum.

Measurable. And teachers need to know what the measurement means. This is usually more of a concern when examining standardized scores. For example, if a student has a RIT score of 230, is that student above or below where he/she should be? Last year that same student had a RIT score of 220. Is growth of 10 points over one year excellent, average or poor? If a student has a Lexile score of 800, what does that mean? Teachers need to know how different measurements measure up.

In addition to the data itself, a school should provide teachers with the following resources:

A model for collecting and using data. Often, it is not a matter of teachers not wanting to use data; they just don't know how to collect and use it. Unfortunately, most graduate-level courses that focus on the collection and use of data are designed for people who are going to publish or prepare for a dissertation. In other words, it isimpractical for everyday classroom use. One good alternative is finding teachers on staff who already use classroom data in such a way that the whole staff could benefit from learning their methods. There are also many professional videos portraying data collection in "live" classrooms.

A method to share data. There are many ways to share data. The most obvious place would be with a course-alike or small group. Some schools have a "data wall" or "war room" where teachers can post classroom data for other teachers to see what they are doing. We are in the process of creating our own data room during this academic year. Results can also be shared at staff development meetings or in a weekly newsletter. The biggest obstacle is the tradition of teachers keeping successes to themselves so they do not come across as being a "know-it-all."

Support and resources for teachers' actions based on the data. When a teacher discovers a successful activity in class, he or she should share it with the rest of the staff. Sharing results can be very rewarding and can help in the development of a professional learning community. It is also another way to encourage other teachers to use data collection in their classroom.

Support and resources for data-based action. Once teachers start analyzing data, questions will arise. They may have concerns about the way they collected the data, they might need help with a problem they are having collecting the data, or they might want some help analyzing data. In many cases data analysis brings more questions than answers. Why did some students learn a concept and not others? Why is a certain group struggling with a particular idea? As these questions arise, teachers need support to help them find the answers they seek.

School districts—from superintendents to principals to classroom teachers—are being held ever more accountable for what students learn and do not learn. The days of teachers hiding their instruction and its results behind a closed door are over. Collaborating as a staff to collect and analyze classroom data is a giant step toward success.

Chapter 11

Soon after our initial study of the learning model, the science department began looking at the best way to implement the three-step learning model. Our administrative promise had been that students would improve and we would not work harder. Thanks to science department's early efforts, the students certainly improved. The part about not working harder, however, eventually became a problem. But what we learned from their initial foray into the learning model set the stage for us as a school. We found more questions rather than an immediate answer, but they were good questions that we had not even asked before.

Science Department/Biology

CARL WEAVER AND CHRIS WEAVER, SCIENCE TEACHERS

Over the past 36 years, Goshen High School has grown from a school of 750 students to a school of over 1700 students. The science department has expanded from four teachers offering four basic courses to a department of 12 teachers offering 12 different courses. Early on, the four teachers functioned as "independent contractors," with little or no collaboration. As the multiple teachers began teaching the same courses, the possibility and the need for collaboration grew. As early as 20 years ago, biology teachers and chemistry teachers started meeting in "course-alike" groups to make decisions about curriculum, pacing, and assessment. Those early meetings did not include any discussion about *essential learnings* or *remediation* and rarely resulted in giving the same assessment.

About 15 years ago the biology teachers made a stronger effort to develop common assessments. They developed objective tests for all biology students at the end of each chapter. Curriculum pacing became extremely important also as students began to switch teachers at semester due to the demands of a growing master schedule. The biology teachers tried very hard to teach at the same pace and to test at the same time, including activities like labs. The goal was to give biology students an equal experience regardless of which teacher they had.

Upper level science students really desiring to challenge themselves can become part of the school's model rocket club. The efforts of this club have been rewarded with high finishes in national competitions. These students have made remote presentations viewed by NASA scientists. They have created payloads and measured the effect of the launch. The teacher, Ken Horst, has been published in national periodicals on several occasions. Each year, new challenges grow out of this project as students continue to build their expertise.

Until several years ago fewer than 50 percent of the incoming freshmen took biology, with the remaining students enrolling in an introductory science course. Freshmen enrollment in biology has increased for the last several years to the point where now 100 percent of the incoming freshmen take biology. This has broadened the spectrum of student ability and increased the number of biology sections and teachers, both of which have increased the need for course-alike collaboration. A second influencing factor has been the increased emphasis on state standards. A third influencing factor has been the increased emphasis on the learning model at GHS.

During the 2002-2003 school year the biology department numbered six teachers who covered 19 sections and approximately 475 students. By this time, common assessment tests had evolved to include both objective questions (multiple choice, matching, etc.) graded by a scanning machine, and short answer and essay questions graded by individual teachers. Teachers noticed an ever-expanding gap between the high achieving students and the low achieving students on common assessments, due mostly to the increasing heterogeneity in the classroom. In an effort to meet the needs of an increasingly diverse biology student population as well as follow the learning model, teachers implemented a "tutorial-enrichment" program.

The tutorial-enrichment program was carried out on Monday's since that was a traditional 50-minute class period. The team of biology teachers agreed to divide the task of developing tutorial and enrichment activities for each of the chapters studied. Each teacher determined which students in their classes needed remediation and which students were eligible for enrichment. This division was generally based on the students' performance on the previous assessment. In some cases students requested a tutorial assignment and this was granted.

At least two sections of biology meet during all seven periods of the school day. For each class period, teachers decided who would be in charge of the separate rooms for tutorial and enrichment, and students were sent to the corresponding classroom. The tutorial sessions were used to re-teach and reinforce content from the previous unit and weak areas from the previous test, as well as study skills and test-taking skills. The enrichment sessions were intended to find interesting activities and applications of the previous material that would push students beyond the normal expectations for that unit.

We did not collect large amounts of quantitative data as to whether or not the program was successful in reducing the achievement gap. Generally, we felt it was successful in improving the performance of lower achieving students and enhancing the learning experience of the higher achieving students. Our data followed several of the lower performing students and documented their improved performances on the end of unit tests.

One drawback to the program was that it did not reduce the teacher to student ratio and therefore the tutorial sessions were very demanding on the teacher. A second drawback was that it required tremendous amounts of extra preparation time to prepare extra activities along with the regular curriculum. A third drawback was that it took 25 percent of our weekly class time, slowing our progress through the prescribed curriculum. Finally, at this stage in implementing the learning model, biology teachers had not yet worked on essential learnings for each chapter, so it was not always clear exactly what we needed to remediate.

With the advent of the freshman academy that focused on lower-to-middle achieving students and the restructuring of Student Resource Time (SRT) in 2003-2004, the decision was made to work at tutorial and enrichment activities during SRT in the resource room. The focus of course-alike meetings now shifted to working with the state standards and our own standards to determine essential learnings for each chapter. We also aligned our common assessments with the essential learnings.

Marine Biology

The Marine Biology program began in 1974 along with a new Biology II course, both of which were offered as an effort to increase upper-level science offerings at GHS. I had taken Marine Biology in Florida while in college, and I thought a similar course would fit will with high school curriculum. I soon discussed this plan with the high school principal, the superintendent of schools, and the school board.

All levels of the administration initially had questions about my rationale for doing a remote study. My students and I worked on objectives for a marine biology study in the Florida Keys and were given audience at a school board meeting in the fall of 1974. After many questions about safety, transportation, lodging, curriculum, and costs, the matter was unanimously approved by the board. It was the first out-of-state of field trip in the history of Goshen High School, taking us 1500 miles to the Florida Keys.

The 1974 trip included 23 students and adults and occurred during the Christmas break. Our initial studies were conducted at Lime Tree Bay Motel in Layton on Long Key. Because of the success of this first trip, the program has continued for 32 years and has expanded to include as many as 102 people. Two changes, however, are that the trip is now over spring break to take advantage of warmer water temperatures, and the duration of the trip has been expanded from seven days to ten. Since that initial trip, the school board has granted up to two days of missed class time to allow for the 10-day trip. The program has also changed its home base several times during the 32 years, moving from Lime Tree Bay Motel, to Star of the Sea Motel, to Hawk's Cay Resort.

Marine Biology is a one-semester accredited course as part of the science curriculum, but it is offered outside of the school day. Students attend several pre-trip seminars, held evenings and Saturdays before spring break. During these seminars, they are introduced to marine biology, marine chemistry, and marine ecology. They practice tasks that they will need to do on location. Once in Florida, students attend daily seminars on the animal and plant groups. They take daily excursions to different identified marine habitats and study the flora and fauna of each. During these excursions they work at identifying and classifying marine organisms as well as completing chemical profiles of water quality. All of their findings are then recorded in a marine biology workbook. Working in groups, they prepare an exit project detailing one of the habitats, which they present to the group at the conclusion of the week. Upon returning to Goshen, they complete a two-hour exam and a written evaluation of the experience.

Students who participate in this program are generally juniors and seniors, although in recent years we have included some exceptional freshmen and sophomores. The students have generally completed courses in biology and chemistry as well as one more upper-level science course; Marine Biology requires a lot of work, and is only offered during a vacation, so the students enrolled are generally very science-serious. In fact, a number of former GHS students are now in marine biology careers.

This program has continued for 32 years because of the tremendous support from the school community as well as the Goshen community. I have tried to maintain a 2-to-1 ratio of students to adults on this trip. This requires a large number of chaperones to accompany the students. Many of these chaperones have been other faculty and staff members from Goshen Community Schools. Others have been interested parents of students or other people from the community, including medical personnel.

Students are required to finance their own way or apply for financial aid to go on the trip. In the latter case, I have sometimes solicited donations from the community. In addition to financial aid, community members have contributed needed supplies, including two boats over the course of 32 years. The current boat is a 27-foot pontoon boat donated in 1999. I have also received excellent cooperation from the students involved, which is what has really allowed the program to be successful for students and teachers for so many years.
-CARL WEAVER

To study the progress of our students and examine the validity of our tests, we conducted item analyses on the objective portions of our tests. Questions missed by more than 40% of our students were examined closely to determine whether the question was poor or whether we did a poor job of teaching the concept. This involved the comparison of individual teacher data. Initially, this was very threatening to teachers. We were able to overcome some of this by realizing that averages always vary from class to class for a variety of reasons. We kept the emphasis on improving teaching and helping students, not on evaluating individual teachers.

Although direct teacher comparisons were not done, the process allowed the individual teachers to learn a lot from each other and to talk about improved ways to teach specific concepts.

Even with the freshmen academy and the efforts at enrichment it became apparent that the gap between students in biology was just too large to handle in one classroom. The decision was made to implement honors biology for the 2004-2005 school year. These students were selected based on a recommendation by their middle school science teachers as well as achievement test scores.

During the 2004-2005 school year the biology teachers continued to meet weekly. These meetings involved academy, regular, and honors level teachers, all of whom use the same textbook. We used the meetings to determine essential learnings and create assessments that reflected them. Teachers also developed labs and activities to help students master the essential learnings. The task of developing and prepping these activities was divided among all the teachers.

With the three levels of biology meeting together, pacing became a real issue. One possible solution to this problem is that the honors biology teachers will soon form their own course-alike group and use a different textbook.

During the past two years we have focused heavily on the first two steps of the learning model: determining essential learnings and assessing the students' mastery of them. In an effort to pay more attention to the final step of the learning model, next year's honors biology courses have been aligned with the freshman academy biology courses during the same class period. The plan is to provide opportunities for academy students to be tutored by honors students. During the upcoming 2005-2006 school year, the science department will have six different course-alike groups functioning.

As stated above, several of these have been active for many years, even before there was an emphasis at GHS on course-alike and the learning model. We will continue to focus on essential learning, developing effective classroom activities, and producing valid common assessments. We feel that we do not yet do an adequate job of dealing with students who do not succeed on the common assessments. In the coming year, we want to improve upon the way we deal with these students as well as continue to develop methods of valid nontraditional assessments.

As we view all that has been done with course-alike meetings and working with the learning model, we can make several observations: more incoming freshmen are being challenged by taking a more rigorous entry-level science course; the academy program allows us to give more help to lower achieving students and has reduced the failure rate; the honors program allows us to raise the bar for higher achieving students; and course-alike meetings have improved our ability to create valid activities and assessments. And we have managed to do all of these things without reducing individual teachers' creativity in the classroom.

CARL WEAVER AND CHRIS WEAVER

Chapter 12

The learning model system works most readily in departments with multiple sections and teachers of a single class. For example, the Algebra teachers can get together in their course-alike groups and use common assessments to gauge student progress and plan the follow-up interventions. Working in departments without multiple teachers creates another challenge. The following is the Foreign Language Department's initial steps with the learning model.

Using Essential Learnings to Guide Instruction and Assessment in German

JIM GRAVES AND CHAD COLLINS, GERMAN

Three years ago our school began talking about ways in which we could decrease the number of students with failing grades and push more successful students into upper level classes. During the summer of 2004 we decided that it was time for us to make some changes in the way we assessed students' learning and also begin to do more with the results of assessments rather than simply moan that students weren't working to their full potential.

At first we decided to make changes because we felt we were being steered in that direction by our administration, plus we wanted to feel like we were doing our part to help improve our school. Later, our desire to work for change really began in earnest when we attended HOPE conferences in the spring and summer of 2004 and learned what it meant to "be on board." We realized that even though we always really wanted to help students improve based on the information we gained from periodic assessments, the problem was that we were unsure of what to do with that information. We always felt rushed for time, and it felt nearly impossible to take time after a test to re-teach topics students evidently had not grasped the first time.

The most important discovery we made from listening to our administrators and to the presenters at the HOPE conference was that meaningful assessment must occur often, be short and succinct, and allow time for the instructor to act upon the results of the assessment. Testing students at the end of a unit is simply too late. Assessment needs to happen continually along the way so that meaningful remediation can occur. We also learned that the instructor must establish the most important ideas, or essential learnings, to be taught during each unit. The assessment tools must then measure students' proficiency in these essential learnings. With these two ideas in mind, we set out to change the way we were assessing our students' learning.

For each unit we established anywhere from 5-10 essential learnings, though it is important to remember that establishing essential learnings does not mean that we taught nothing else. We did not dilute our instruction, we simply identified those topics based on the state standards and our own personal experiences. For each of the 5-10 essential learnings, we then developed a short assessment tool. To do this, we used a variety of formats: multiple choice, short answer, listening, and oral assessments. It was very important to work with students when this project began and convince them that all students learn at different rates and that being required to do remediation did not reflect in any way one's own level of intelligence.

We teach German levels I-V and use a combination of textbooks, videos, recordings and various other materials of our own that we have developed over the years. We were initially afraid that revising the way we assess students' learning would involve developing countless new tests and quizzes. This was true, to a certain degree, but we also made every attempt to make use of assessment tools that were already available to us. Our assessments usually had 5-10 questions and assessed only one essential learning. Because these learnings are at the core of what we teach and mastery of the topics is imperative, we set a benchmark for all assessments of 80 percent. This means that any student not scoring at least 80 percent on an assessment would be given additional help and assessed again until his or her score reached the benchmark. This required students to do remediation before or after school, online, with a peer group and tutor, or during our school's Student Resource Time (SRT) period. Students could also elect to study on their own before re-taking the assessment. A sample set of essential learnings and their corresponding assessments for a unit in beginning German and in German III are listed below.

German I Unit Essential Learnings and Assessments
Vorschau
-Geography: location, names, and capitals of German-speaking countries.
-Written Quiz
-Alphabet
-Oral Quiz on paper
-Introductions
      -Oral Quiz in class (ask all students and give check)
-Numbers 0-20
-Oral Quiz on paper
-Basic items in a classroom

-Written Quiz
-TPR of classroom directions
    -Students quiz each other with rubric and tape recorder

German III Unit Essential Learnings and Assessments

Karneval Unit

-Vocabulary and reading comprehension associated with reading texts (p. 241 and 243)
    -Multiple Choice quiz over text and vocabulary for *Fasnacht inBasel*
-Multiple Choice quiz over text and vocabulary for *Wie kommen wir im Künstlerhaus?*
-Holidays in German-speaking countries
-Written quiz on holidays
-Narrative past of weak, strong, and irregular weak verbs and modals
-Weak Narrative Past written quiz
-Strong Narrative Past written quiz
-Modal verb Narrative Past written quiz
-Adjective endings with definite articles
-Written quiz

At the end of each unit we still gave a test. We used parts of our earlier unit tests, but some modifications were required. First, 80 percent of the unit tests now assess the essential learnings materials. The remaining 20 percent assesses other topics from a unit but which are not necessarily one of the essential learnings. Second, we also made sure that the unit tests measure what we actually teach, meaning we do not trick or surprise students with questions about material we never discussed. Third, students who have not yet achieved the 80 percent benchmark on the essential learnings assessments are not allowed to take the unit test until they are ready. It suddenly seemed ridiculous to have students who had not yet shown mastery of the essential materials take the unit assessment just because the rest of the class was doing so.

We experienced several positives changes as a result of our efforts during the past school year. We discovered that our outlook on teaching changed. We began to be much more careful in our instruction the first time around. We felt that it was important for students to be successful as quickly as possible and assure that they would be able to reach the 80 percent benchmark of the quiz the first time. We began to be very aware of the sequence of our instruction and the opportunities we gave students for practice.

Advance College Placement

At registration time I recently overheard a student say, "You have to take Writing Analytically (W131). It's hard but it really taught me how to write." The word is out! Students want to be challenged. They are proud of being successful in a course that uses a college textbook and demands much of them intellectually. Getting college credit at a reduced cost is also a real bonus. Enrollment in our two English Advance College Placement courses is growing because the curriculum for these courses is excellent, teachers are well trained, and certainly not least our guidance department is encouraging students to take more challenging classes.

Our advanced students have opportunities to take a variety of courses for high school and college credit concurrently. Through Advance College Placement (ACP) students may receive dual credit for courses in the English, history/social studies, science, math, and foreign language departments. Students who complete the courses with a C or higher receive college credit that may be transferred to many colleges and universities throughout the state and across the country. This credit is offered through Indiana University.

To teach an ACP course, teachers are required to complete about 40 hours of training on the Indiana University Bloomington campus during the summer. In addition, IU expects teachers to attend a day of in-service each year for each ACP course they teach.

In the English department, we decided to offer an ACP course about 8 years ago. Our original purpose in offering ACP was to offer a writing course that was challenging for our top students. We felt that one of our current writing classes didn't require enough writing and didn't prepare the students for college-level writing as well as it should. Currently we offer two ACP courses (writing and literature) that juniors or seniors may take, and we have four teachers trained to teach these courses. Not all students who enroll in the classes opt to take them for dual credit; however, all benefit from the increased rigor these classes offer.

Our enrollment in ACP has continued to grow, especially in the writing class (W131). When we began offering W131, we had two sections. Several years ago we added a third section and this year for the first time we will offer four sections. In the English department we have about 70 students taking ACP courses for dual credit each year.

Recently a former student returned from college to attend a school event. He had taken W131 for dual credit. So far in college he had written 4 papers and earned A's on all of them! "I'm glad I got my papers ripped apart in high school," he said. High expectations benefit all students, and students come to expect and appreciate that much is expected of them.
-MARILYN GRABER

As the year progressed and students became more aware and comfortable with the system of essential learnings and assessments, we noticed that students worked harder in preparation for the first assessment over an essential learning. Students in the German III class even began to request and attend review sessions to prepare for the quiz before it was given the first time. They expressed an interest in being proactive instead of waiting to fail the assessment and then doing remediation.

The establishment of essential learnings makes very clear for the teacher and students what is expected and what will eventually appear on a unit test. Students have already been assessed in a more abbreviated fashion over every main concept on the unit test. In the past, we felt that everything we had ever mentioned in class was important and so the unit tests were actually more random because a single test could never cover everything that had been presented during the unit. In a survey given to students at the end of the year asking them to reflect on the changes we had made, 112 out of 123 students either agreed or strongly agreed that the essential learnings matched the material on unit tests.

Finally, establishing essential learnings, assessing students' knowledge, and remediating before the unit test helps students realize their proficiency or deficiency in specific areas of the course and build confidence. They are usually pretty sure how they will perform based on their scores on the smaller assessments of each essential learning for the unit. For example, at the end of one grading period we felt rushed and announced to students that the final two essential learnings for that unit would not be assessed. Many students became visibly agitated and proclaimed that they would be ill-prepared for the unit test if they didn't have the opportunity to be assessed on the two essential learnings and remediate any problems the assessment might indicate. On the same above-mentioned survey, 104 out of 124 students agreed or strongly agreed that the system of setting essential learnings and taking quizzes until a minimum score was achieved helped improve their knowledge and performance.

As the year progressed we also experienced our share of frustrations. One challenge was that when it came time for the unit test, not all students were ready to take it. With various students at differing levels of readiness for the test, test time became chaotic. Some students also began to use this as an excuse to procrastinate. An additional challenge was making sure that students met the benchmark on each assessment. This often was a daunting bookkeeping task considering each unit had 5 – 10 assessments, there were multiple levels of German, and possibly 140 students, some of whom wanted to avoid re-taking assessments. Perhaps the most serious problem was that of students failing to take remediation and assessments seriously. Some students would refuse to study or review a difficult concept and insist on quickly re-taking the quiz. Inevitably they would fail and be forced to re-take the quiz again, leading to previously mentioned problems at test times.

For next year, we envision several changes that we hope will improve on last year's transformation. One change we hope to make is the way we do remediation. Remediation is actually just another way to allow more time to learn for students who need it. Most students who need remediation simply need another chance to interact with the materials and concepts. We feel this additional interaction does not need to be complex, lengthy, or flashy. We also want to explore varied means of presenting the material, such as online tutorials, hand-outs, and peer tutoring. It is important to remember, though, that the way we do remediation needs to be structured so that students view it as actually being of help to them. According to the end of the year survey, students indicated that they prefer working by themselves or with the teacher or peers to get extra help.

Another change we have considered is lowering the benchmark to 70 or 75 percent. This came as a result of comments from colleagues, self-doubt, and occasional weak performance on essential learning assessments. However, in the end of year survey, 83 out of 125 students either strongly disagreed or disagreed that it would be good to lower the benchmark for quizzes to 75 percent. Eighty percent of students in German III, an upper-level course where students faced even more challenging material on the learning assessments, answered that they strongly disagreed or disagreed with lowering the benchmark for quizzes to 75 percent. One student even suggested raising the benchmark in order to ensure success.

Yet another change we would like to implement is a set of guidelines for determining a specific amount of time during which a student must complete re-taking quizzes and take the unit test. This would ensure that students are not allowed to procrastinate in taking a unit test.

While this project has often meant additional work and effort, it has also offered us as educators the chance to think deeply about what we really teach and why we teach it. We feel it has positively influenced our students' learning and for that reason we will continue to attempt to improve the work we have begun in order to make sure that all students are given the opportunity to learn in spite of their abilities or performance levels.

Chapter 13

Outlined in the first chapter of this section of this book is Freshmen Academy, one of the interventions used for identified freshmen. The ninth grade English teachers have taken this process a bit further for all ninth grade students. Representatives from ninth grade English get together each year with other schools from our athletic/academic conference to discuss standards and how to incorporate them into our curriculum. These meetings, along with departmental release time, have brought about considerable growth in our students. These intra-department conversations and inter-school conversations have been integral in their journey for student improvement.

English

ANDRÉ SWARTLEY AND SCOTT GARVIN, ENGLISH

Obstacles to Change

The most obvious obstacle to change is routine. Such a statement may seem overly simple, but teachers embedded in routine are powerful in their resistance. The following are two of a teacher's best weapons at the onset of change:

"They did this a decade ago and a year later it was gone. I'm not doing extra work that won't even matter next September."

"I've been doing the same thing for twenty years and *it works*."

These ideas are seductive because of the truth in them. Chances are an administrator *did* introduce a similar idea ten years ago, but because of other pressures abandoned it before it became standard practice. Chances are a twenty-year veteran of teaching *has* been successful after two decades of refining curriculum.

And as long as we're being honest, administrators are not credible as instigators of curricular change because they are no longer in the classroom. However, administrators are the ones who present the new ideas; teachers with more than a year or two of experience are rarely compelled to change what they do, and veteran teachers can quickly persuade the rookies that teaching is plenty hard without paying attention to administrators' screwball ideas. This thought process takes no time or initiative to create but is almost unstoppable once it starts.

Principals at Goshen High School solved this problem by breaking the faculty into smaller groups. One or two principals sitting at a round table with the English 9 teachers is a more open setting for dialogue than a full meeting of nearly 100 staff members. And dialogue is the key. The administrators tossed out a few ideas about common assessments for ninth graders and a more defined focus on standards and then let us, the teachers, hash out the particulars. They allowed us to orchestrate—and therefore own—the changes rather than having new "requirements" thrust at us. Just like in the classroom, a little psychology goes a long way.

A third comment teachers make is: "I have to plan and grade on my own time already, and they expect me to add this on top of everything else?" (We teachers are cat-like in our need to hack up these messy hairballs before continuing our jobs.) Once again, there is truth in this gripe, but the administrators doused the fire easily enough. "If the issue is time," they said, "here's some more." The English 9 course-alike group was granted professional leave to re-write curriculum, create common assessments, and align each unit of study to the state standards to make sure we did not forget any. The logic is simple: more work means more time, and that time has to come from somewhere.

Essential Learnings

Identifying essential learnings means never having to say, "Because I've always done it this way." The English 9 course-alike group met over the summer and during the school year to trim any fat from our units...there wasn't much. We sat down with the Indiana State Standards, returned portions of the Graduation Qualifying Exam (GQE) exams, and several burbling coffee makers and decided which standards our state deemed most important. The good news is that the standards are idiotically vague. Things like, "Students should learn to interpret age-appropriate literature." And textbook companies have made their billions telling us what "age-appropriate" means: freshmen should read *Romeo and Juliet*, sophomores should read *A Midsummer Night's Dream*, and so on. Studying the standards basically kept us honest with all levels of freshmen English; the English 9 students have to meet the same standards in one year as the honors and Gifted/Talented students.

Common Assessments and Item Analyses

An early concern we had with establishing common assessments was that we would simply start teaching to the test, therefore eliminating any need or opportunity for teachers' individual creativity. We agreed immediately that all ninth grade teachers could teach the essential learnings in any way that was appropriate and effective for their classes. For example, one teacher may have to devise two different lessons on a single concept to meet the needs of two freshman classes. Requiring common lesson plans would be ludicrous and self-destructive.

A second concern developed quickly as well. No one had used the words *merit pay,* but we saw them on the horizon anyway. After all, one benefit of common assessments is the item analysis, which is basically a graph showing how every student scored on every test question. Such graphs could easily be displayed on an overhead projector or in a PowerPoint presentation for the faculty. Such graphs could be used to determine the effectiveness of any single teacher or department. Initially, we only had our principals' promises not to use the item analyses for evil.

We need not have worried. The item analyses are usually confined to course-alike groups. They are useful in determining which concepts were difficult for students; which questions, if any, were ineffective; and, yes, which teachers had difficulty conveying certain concepts. We had to get over our own egos, but course-alike groups are small and consistent and non-threatening. Mr. D will never celebrate the failure of Mr. S because it makes him look good. Instead, common assessments have united us to be successful as a department instead of individuals.

The Media Center – Another Piece of the Puzzle

The media center is a very busy place, and we wouldn't want it any other way. Our circulation statistics have been on a steady climb for the past four years. On a typical day, we'll see around 200 of our students using the facility and its resources. We're a definite part of both the instructional and learning processes in our building.

I often collaborate with teachers in their course-alike groups. I move in and out of the course-alike groups based on when different classes are incorporating information literacy and/or projects into their curricula. For example, I work closely with the teachers in the 10th grade English course-alike group – particularly for the persuasion unit. Leading up to this unit, I meet regularly with their group and participate in the discussion and planning of the unit. When the time for the unit arrives, I often also teach; we work with finding, evaluating, and citing sources. During the unit, the course-alike group allows for discussion. We can talk about what some kids are struggling with and what has worked for some teachers. We can also make plans for improvement for the next group of kids entering into the unit, since we have to stagger the sections over almost the entire semester because there are too many sections to do all at once.

I also collaborate closely with the ENL teachers. Collaboration with this department works in the same way; we plan ahead of time, share the teaching, and work with another on many projects throughout the year. I feel like my work with the ENL classes is really important since many of those students will soon be mainstreamed into science, social studies, and English classes, and they have a much better chance of being successful in those classes if they enter them with strong information literacy skills. The language provides enough difficulty without having to worry about proficient skills in finding, evaluating, and using both print and electronic materials. We also work on integrating and teaching technology as well. We try to prepare the kids for further work in word processing, PowerPoint, Publisher, and Excel as these applications are successfully integrated into many assignments across the curriculum in our school.

SRT seems to be a critical part of the learning model, since this period of the day provides some students the extra time they need in order to be successful. The media center is one of the resource rooms during SRT. Students can be assigned here and attendance is taken - just like any of the other resource rooms in the building. It would be very typical for us to see anywhere between 50-100 students during each 45 minute section of the SRT block. Students use the time to research and create and finish projects. They might also work on PLATO. They might be working on a group projects. They're doing whatever they need to do in order to successful in their classes. We provide plenty of individual help during this time. It's a hectic time of the day because there are so many kids working on so many different things; however, when all goes well, it's also a very productive time of the day.

Our school has done much work on streamlining the students' transition between the middle school and high school, and our area has also been including in that process. When students are in Family and Consumer Science classes at GMS, they visit our building and are introduced to several different areas and how things work there. One of their visits is dedicated to spending a block of time in the media center. I give a brief introduction and then have a short activity for them that gets them up and moving. As they are completing the activity, they can easily see what the high school students are working on and what's expected of them. The media center is also a stop during their tour on Freshmen Orientation Day and then we do further orientation work in 9th Grade English classes during the first few weeks of the school year.

I also keep the learning model in mind when I work on collection development. The collection represents many different reading levels – both at the enrichment and remediation levels. It's also extremely diverse and represents many different viewpoints. It's current and accurate and is weeded regularly. It must stay appealing in order for the kids to continue to use and thrive in print resources. We also subscribe to several electronic resources and then use the Internet to round out the research process.

In closing, I like to think of the media center as one of the smaller learning communities present in our building. We only have two people staffing the area during the school day, and we get to know as many of our 1700+ students as we can. Kids know that they can count on us to help them in any way we're able. When kids need more time in order to be successful, we are often a safety net and there to help them with their projects. We also have a core group of kids that rely on the library as a safe, comfortable, and welcoming place in our building for the time before school, during lunch, and after school. Many recent studies show that a strong media program can improve students' scores on standardized tests, and we take that very seriously. We are continually looking for ways to help as another piece of the puzzle in improving student achievement.
-THERESA COLLINS, Media Specialist

Evolving Common Assessments

As helpful as common assessments have been, we have already been forced to change them because no successful educational practice can remain stagnant. Initially common assessments followed standards so closely that sections of the test were numbered to match the standard numbers in the state handbook. The students who performed poorly on our common assessments fared little better on the state's tests, so we cosmetically altered the common assessments to look like the ISTEP and GQE. Specifically, a boxed reading selection was at the top of each page and students answered five to six questions about the reading, all multiple-choice, on the same page. Selections could come from texts the students had seen (as with *Romeo & Juliet*) or brand new sources (as with Short Fiction, Poetry, and Nonfiction). Format was no longer a problem, but with so many reading selections the tests became unbearably long.

On to the next mutation: no English teacher wanted every test to consist of, say, ten reading selections and sixty multiple choice questions. Easy grading aside, such a test cannot measure all that we want the students to learn. We decided a common assessment could be just a portion of a test instead of the whole thing. Currently, common assessments for any unit are limited to 40 questions, and teachers can fill out tests with additional questions as they choose. Common assessments changed yet again during the past school year. Our administrators dredged Bloom's Taxonomy from a sinkhole in the growing mire of educational research, and it was a good thing they did; Bloom's forced us to think doubly hard about every question on our tests. We couldn't just say, "Yes, this is a good question," and move on, even if it was true.

Every question had to fall into one of the six levels of Bloom's Taxonomy, and there had to be a balanced number of each. (Most standardized tests do not move past the second level of Bloom's, but if higher test scores were our only concern we could simply serve the students ISTEP-prep catalogues all year.) Once all the teachers in the course-alike group agreed that we had good questions that fit where they belonged, we had developed some fantastic tests. Just ask the kids.

Analysis and Beyond

Good units, good planning, good tests...so what? Common assessments would only be effective if we used the results to facilitate learning. As stated above, we pooled our results for each test. We expected a larger number of students to have trouble with the higher functions in Bloom's Taxonomy, and they did, but they frequently missed the same lower-level questions as well. We were left with the question: Did we write bad questions or fail to teach the concepts? (At GHS, students' apathy is no excuse for students *or* teachers.) And we make the appropriate changes, usually re-teaching concepts.

Unfortunately, we rarely have class time to re-teach even small portions of a unit after the exam, but our school has created extra time in the form of SRT. During this time students may request extra help in any subject, and those who need help but do not request it can be assigned to a resource room by a teacher. Every department has its own resource room with a trained teacher or two in residence. Students who do not need one-on-one help may complete homework in a homeroom assigned for all four years. Finally, the school's library and computer labs are open for computer-based remediation specifically tooled to aid GQE retakes. The philosophy at Goshen High School is that students do not have the option to fail. If they struggle we give them more time, more time, more time...

Continuing Change

While common assessments have helped considerably with lower-achieving students, our top students test well no matter what we put in front of them. They should not receive less attention because they excel. The next step for our department is common essay assessments. For example, three teachers currently teach English 10 Honors. They cover the same material at roughly the same pace as each other, and have objective (multiple choice) common assessments.

The Stratford Experience

Generating enthusiasm and excellence in reading and understanding literature extends well beyond the classroom at GHS. Since 1978 the English department has taken students to the Stratford Festival in Ontario, Canada, one of the premier repertory theaters on the North American continent. In 1985 the field trip was developed into a for-credit literature course in our elective program and it continues to be a class enthusiastically supported by students, faculty and administration.

The first trip included three required and two optional plays, five teachers, some other parents and friends, and about 20 students. Today we have expanded to include ten English teachers who divide the teaching, grading, and administrative duties, and about 40 juniors and seniors. We now see five plays, generally two Shakespearean plays, one musical, and two other productions of dramatic import. The content of the class changes annually, of course, as the season changes at Stratford.

Students read and study the plays before the trip that we take over fall break (Thursday-Sunday) in the final week of October. During class sessions, which are held both during and outside the regular school day, we discuss the works and also how plays can be interpreted on stage. We learn the historical background and social milieu of the playwrights and plays. We study the history of theater and the types of plays produced that particular season at Stratford. Students complete and present projects, write papers, act scenes, listen to lectures, research, journal, discuss, take quizzes, and finish course work in early November after the trip with a comprehensive final exam and major culminating project.

Of course, the trip itself is the high point of the class. Besides experiencing the plays, while in Stratford we tour the costume warehouse or backstage areas, participate in a "chat" with actors either before or after a production, and sometimes enjoy a seminar on a topic such as stage combat. The education office at the Festival is generous with resources and help in scheduling the extras. The talent, creativity, and professionalism of the repertory company excite and completely enthrall our students; the literature comes alive in a way that cannot be duplicated in the classroom or on the screen. The impact of seeing these fine productions cannot be overstated. I believe our school's excellent drama productions have benefited from our students being exposed to such outstanding theater. Students come back into the traditional literature classroom with a renewed appreciation of the enjoyment and learning available through reading, discussing, and understanding literature generally and dramatic literature specifically. Teachers and students benefit from the relationships we build as we travel together. Additionally, it is an expanding experience for our students to visit another country and city. They recognize and appreciate significant cultural differences between our two countries and towns.

Class expectations have grown over the years, but enthusiasm has not waned as evidenced by our yearly waiting lists of students who wish to participate. We are proud of this program as it inspires students and teachers to experience the joy of dramatic literature firsthand.
-SUE NEEB—English

One plan is to create common rubrics for a few essay questions per test and then compare results. Another is to shuffle all essays from a test into a pile and distribute them evenly among the three teachers. This second option would help twofold—students could receive feedback from three sources instead of one, and the teachers could test their own grading consistency. Freshmen courses will have common assessments for every unit within a year; we have aimed to create one per semester since the program started.

Every teacher on the English 9 course-alike team would agree that the tests are better because of our scrutiny and for having built them together. Sure, we have had to change the existing tests each year, but we should do that anyway; students are never the same from year to year, so why should we expect the same tests to meet their needs?

Now we can admit that common assessments started out as intimidating, turf-encroaching bugaboos. None of us wanted the work or the responsibilities. Now we're grateful. When the freshman bomb a question we addressed fifty-three times in class, we hear that the same thing happened to our colleagues. We see the problem, discuss the problem, and try to solve the problem. The pressure of working in the most heavily-tested department in the building is still there, but at least we share it.

Chapter 14

How does academic improvement reach beyond the traditional classroom into elective areas? Often these areas are forgotten and pushed aside with the pressures of state expectations and NCLB. Yet we must insist on educating the entire child and this means that elective areas are critical as well. The physical education department has always examined curriculum, but assessing and improving have not been the emphasis. With technology, this can change. Today's students are also an at-risk generation in the area of health that impacts everyone with the spiraling costs of health care. In Indiana, students are only required to take PE one year giving us a very short window to teach about fitness for life. The physical education department is using the learning model to help students improve their own vital statistics and in the process, they are changing how we look at physical education.

Physical Education's Vision for the Future

BARB CARBAUGH, PHYSICAL EDUCATION

It has been the goal of our physical education department for the last decade to change from "Traditional P.E" to what is now labeled the "New P.E." If your physical education teachers are like ours, the writing is on the wall, change needs to take place. It is apparent that our student population is changing and that physical education needs to change to meet their needs. Many of our students are overweight, carry too much body fat, and simply do not get enough exercise outside physical education class.

The quality of the two components of physical education in our students, health related physical fitness and skill related fitness, have dropped dramatically. The health related fitness component—cardiovascular fitness, caloric intake vs. output, etc.—is the component physical education could and should address for the lifelong health and wellbeing of our students. If we can change the health related fitness of our students, we can have a positive lifelong effect on the health and wellness of our students. While the skill related areas are important, effecting change in those areas will not necessarily impact the changes that need to take place in their overall health.

So the question is, how do we make the transition logistically and strategically from "traditional PE" to the "new PE"? First and foremost we had the support of our administration. Once they were on board, we could begin the process of overhauling curriculum and over time purchase the necessary equipment to implement the curriculum. We met with our principal ten years ago and presented the idea of purchasing heart rate monitors so we could individualize the program. Our principal understood how physical education, more so than any other discipline, puts students on display. If a student does not know how to do a math problem, only the teacher and that student are aware of the deficiency. If a student cannot run the mile in the set amount of time, everyone in class knows because that student comes in last or at the back of the pack.

Everyone in class knows who the skilled people are and who the unskilled are. In contrast, heart rate monitors allow all students to work at a pace that is right for them based on their individual heart rate, and therefore can achieve success whether they are athletes or non-athletès. In addition to working at a pace that is right individually, it is also the safest way to have students work out. Our kids are out of shape, and yet in traditional PE students had to meet a generic standard to attain a grade: the mile in x amount of time. Those standards did not take into account any of the physical characteristics of the students. Therefore a student could be attempting to achieve success while working at an intensity level entirely unsafe based on that student's fitness, weight, etc. Using the formula for determining a student's target zone and then grading students on time in the zone is the safest way of having students exercise at safe intensity levels. So, change in terms of equipment began with 48 heart rate monitors.

With our building administration on board and heart monitors in hand, we approached the corporation administrators. We presented the changes we had made with the heart monitors to them and the school board, as well as our vision for the future. We spoke to service organizations giving power point presentations in an attempt to get the message out in the community. We also made a couple presentations at faculty meetings/in-services throughout the years to inform our peers of the vision.

Last year our principal supported our efforts to update our heart rate monitors. We began with 36 (updating is costly and would have to take place over the course of a couple years) and a commitment from the administration to purchase an additional 12 each year until we reach 72. Last year we added 12 more and are now at 48. Once we reach 72, we will re-evaluate our needs and plan accordingly.

With updated heart rate monitors, next on the list is working toward a change in facility (see diagram below).

Fitness Area Needs

50 x 50 Foot Space

Computer Tables			Computer Tables		Teacher Computer	
+	+	X	X	X	X	X
X	X	X	X	X	X	X
X	X	X	X	X	X	X
X	X	X	X	X	X	X
I	I	I	I	I	I	I
I	I					
	O		O		O	

I = 8 Rowers
X = 15 Airdyne Bikes, 2 Recumbent Bikes, 6 Uprights
+ = 2 Stair Masters
0 = 4 Steps
O = Universal Weights

We have the fitness equipment we need as a result of the building project but really have no space to efficiently and effectively use the equipment. With the help of our school nurse, we contacted the local hospital to see if they could administer and fund health fitness appraisals on a trial group of students. After numerous meetings with the "Healthy Generations" staff of Goshen General Hospital, the logistics were worked out and we were ready to begin the study.

The hospital agreed to administer appraisals on 125 freshman physical education students. The testing included a complete blood workup, a lifestyle questionnaire, height, weight, percent body fat, body mass index (BMI), blood pressure, and a total breakdown of cholesterol. In the fall, at the start of the school year, all students in the freshman physical education class were given an information letter to take home to parents explaining the study and the first 125 students to return permission slips would make up our group. We also contacted our local newspaper that placed an article in the section of the paper covering what's happening in local schools.

The test results on the students in the fall supported what we all knew to be true - our students are overweight and out of shape (see below).

Goshen General Hospital

Healthy Generations

Get Fit – Get Healthy

Study involved 125 GHS Freshman Students (fall)

Study involved 118 GHS Freshman Students (spring follow up)

Note: The end of the year results are listed in italics.

Results:

- High Blood Pressure 42% at risk, 26.4% high risk = 68.4 %
- *High Blood Pressure 12.8% at risk, 12.8 % at high risk = 25.6%*
- Diabetes 15.2%
- *Diabetes 12.7%*
- Girls % Body Fat – slightly over 1.9%, overweight 72.2% = 74.1%
- *Girls % Body Fat – slightly over 0%, overweight 67.4% = 67.4%*
- Boys % Body Fat – slightly over 1.4%, overweight 40.0% = 41.4%

- *Boys % Body Fat – slightly over 2.8%, overweight 37.55 = 40.3%*
- HDL Cholesterol – at risk16.9%, high risk 46% = 62.9%
- *HDL Cholesterol – at risk 20.9%, high risk 31.3% = 52.1%*
- Total Cholesterol – at risk 18.5%, high risk 11.3% = 29.8%
- *Total Cholesterol – at risk 16.7%, high risk 12.3% = 29%*

The real question was, "Could physical education, geared toward addressing these issues, bring about positive change?" At the end of the year the students were again tested and we eagerly awaited the results listed above. The data supported our claims that we could indeed help our students become healthier people in the course of the school year.

The included data shows, 68.4% of the students were at risk or high risk in terms of their blood pressure and that the number declined to 25.6% by the end of the school year. We also saw a 6.7% drop in percent body fat in girls. All areas tested showed improvement, some more so than others.

With a plan now in place to facilitate fitness equipment usage, making it more functional and practical, we will now spend time this summer writing the classroom portion of the curriculum. While we did present much of the material this past year to provide support and reinforcement education to the health risk appraisal pre-test results, we did not do extensive curriculum writing until we knew it could be implemented for a longer period of time than simply a one year trial study.

We have looked at several textbooks, which are quite good, but our dilemma is time. There is a fine line to how much material we should cover with students at the expense of time spent in activity. The textbooks get very detailed and we feel we could write a synopsis of the concepts for students covering the main points. We need to make sure we dispense enough information to support the activities we do and at the same time provide enough time in activity to bring about positive change in their health.

The nuts and bolts to the topics we feel should be covered in the classroom can certainly be expanded, but we feel the ones listed are the best choices considering our time restraints.

Curriculum topics

- **Principles of training: overload, progression, specificity**
- **FIT principle: frequency, intensity, time**
- **Heart rate: maximum HR, resting HR, target HR zone**
- **Weight control/Body composition: calories intake vs. output, body mass index, percent body fat.**
- **Health Related Fitness vs. Skill Related Fitness: health related to body composition, cardiovascular fitness and endurance, muscular strength and endurance, flexibility**
- **Skill related fitness: agility, balance, coordination, reaction time, speed, power**
- **Diet/Nutrition—food labels, fiber, fat, cholesterol**

All of the changes mentioned above have enabled us finally to teach the entire curriculum in terms of both physical activity and classroom activity that we envisioned when we started 10 years ago. We plan to continue using the learning model to assess individual progress and prescribe corrective measures. While this is an overview, it is not all we do for physical fitness. We are on a journey, and our journey is to improve the health of our students.

The other concept we have put into place is providing a safe environment for students that normally would not participate in PE class. These students who are self-conscious about their physical appearance have often opted to fail PE rather than participate with others who are more fit. The specialized class focuses on fitness but also includes healthy food preparation and healthy lifestyle. Plans are also in the works for offering additional opportunities for students wanting to continue their progress they have made during their first year of working on fitness.

Chapter 15

With the advent of high stakes testing and accountability, two departments have felt the most pressure—English and mathematics. Early in the school improvement process, the math department accepted the challenge of improving student academic performance. This focus brought the teachers together to plan and increased the rigor of our curriculum. In Indiana, the entry-level course for mathematics is algebra, but our department had moved to this concept prior to the requirements levied by the state. Challenges are daunting with higher expectations because each increment of added expectations requires more and more time to accomplish. It is conventional wisdom that students will do better if you just expect more. The reality is that students will do better if you expect more and provide the support in the areas of additional time and individual attention. For students to be successful in the more rigorous environment, teachers must fully utilize the learning model to constantly assess student progress and then act on the findings. As teachers work together, they will continue to define approaches to assist students. The learning model provides the step of assessing the effectiveness to make our system more efficient.

Mathematics Triathlon

JIM SPEICHER, MATHEMATICS TEACHER AND MATHEMATICS COACH

The Triathlon that the math department faces is as challenging as any race you want to be in. Phase one of this Triathlon consists of the expectations of the No Child Left Behind act passed by President Bush. Phase two of the race consists of state standards and the GQE required test by the State of Indiana. The final challenge of this triathlon is to close the achievement gap.

Three years ago, President George W. Bush signed into law the No Child Left Behind Act (NCLB), which reauthorized the Elementary and Secondary Education Act (ESEA), a law first passed in 1965. The new law reflected an unprecedented, bipartisan commitment to ensuring that all students, regardless of their background, receive a quality education. To reach this goal, NCLB refocused federal education programs on the principles of stronger accountability for results, more choices for parents and students, greater flexibility for states and school districts, and the use of research-based instructional methods.

The challenge we faced was that we had ample evidence that our high schools are not adequately preparing students to compete in the workforce or succeed in the pursuit of higher education. The following charts were published for the fifth annual Reality Check, a 2002 study by Public Agenda and Education Week on the nation's progress in raising academic standards in public schools; it is presented here to give support as to the challenges faced in our secondary educational setting.

We took to heart the following information of general research. In addition to this, we added our own frustration with difficulties in getting students to perform at higher levels, particularly since our student demographics were changing. Working together, we began to set plans into place to get more students to cross that bar of high standards. Even though the state has changed our exam and made it more difficult, we continue to make progress in assisting our students to attain these high expectations.

Question: How would you rate recent job applicants/freshman and sophomore students when it comes to [the following characteristics]? Would you say excellent, good, fair, or poor?

EMPLOYERS

	Excellent	Good	Fair	Poor	Don't Know
Grammar and Spelling	2%	25%	45%	28%	-
Ability to write clearly	3%	23%	45%	28%	-
Work habits, such as being organized and on time	4%	27%	38%	32%	-
Basic Math Skills	2%	30%	42%	21%	5%
Being motivated and conscientious	5%	22%	47%	25%	1%

PROFESSORS

	Excellent	Good	Fair	Poor	Don't Know
Grammar and spelling	2%	24%	46%	27%	1%
Ability to write clearly	2%	23%	49%	26%	-
Work habits, such as being organized and on time	2%	24%	54%	20%	-
Basic math Skills	2%	13%	38%	26%	20%
Being motivated and conscientious	6%	36%	47%	12%	-

Sample: 251 employers and 252 Professors
Methodology: Telephone interview conducted Nov. 9 – Dec. 9, 2001
Note: Percentage may not add to 100 percent because of rounding

QUESTION: How would you rate recent job applicants/freshman and sophomore students when it comes to their ability to use computers? Would you say excellent, good, fair, or poor?

	Professors	Employers
Excellent	26%	18%
Good	55%	52%
Fair	15%	18%
Poor	2%	7%
Don't Know	3%	5%

Sample: 252 professors and 251 employers
Methodology: Telephone interview conducted Nov. 9 – Dec. 9, 2001
Note: Percentages may not add to 100 percent because of rounding

QUESTION: First, in terms of academic achievement, do you think the public schools in the community where you teach generally expect kids to learn too much, too little, or are the expectations about right?

	Too much	Too little	About right	Don't know
1997	2%	66%	28%	4%
2001	3%	47%	44%	6%

Sample: 252 professors
Methodology: Telephone interview conducted Nov. 9 – Dec. 9, 2001
Note: Percentages may not add to 100 percent because of rounding.

Methodology

Telephone interviews were conducted Nov. 9 through Dec. 9, 2001, with national, random samples of 600 K-12 public school students in grades K-12; 600 public school students in middle or high school; 251 employers who make hiring decisions for employees recently out of high school or college; and 252 professors at two and four year colleges who taught freshmen or sophomores in the past two years. The margin of error for teachers, parents, and students is plus or minus 4 percentage points; for employers and professors, plus or minus 6 percentage points.

An alarming statistic from this survey was that students who do not complete high school face a lifetime of lowered expectations, a lower income, and a greater chance of being unemployed. For example in 2000, the average full-time annual earnings of a male high school graduate were $36,770, compared to $28,832 for a non-graduate and $26, 692 for a worker with an eighth-grade education. The benefits of college were even more striking, with male college graduates earning almost $78,000 annually.

The NCLB act has led Goshen into a smaller learning communities grant that has pointed our school in the direction of what we like to call a School of One. From this school-wide idea we have tried to apply it to our math department and become a course of one. We meet as course-alike groups to try to teach, assess, evaluate and change our instructional strategies as to best meet the needs of all of our students. It is from these meetings and discussions that we feel we have been able to begin an attack upon our second phase of the triathlon we face that is state standards and the GQE required test by the State of Indiana. This has not been an easy road to navigate, nor has it been without bumps and ruts. Each year we assess student progress and try to best intervene for them, particularly in gaining the necessary skills to master Algebra I.

The following is taken from the Indiana Department of Education website. "The world is changing quickly. In order for students to succeed in school, at work, and in the community, they will need more skills and knowledge than ever before. To meet these challenges, Indiana established world-class academic standards in English/language arts, mathematics, science, and social studies. These standards outline what students should know and be able to do at each grade level." The challenge that we accepted in our department was to be able to address the standards set forth by the state, continue our own high level of expectation at the Algebra I level while trying close our achievement gap.

We have included the standards for Algebra I to show the expansiveness and width of the world-class mathematics standards of Indiana, and to give evidence of why as a department, we had to prioritize some of the standards as to what are the essential skills of an Algebra I course. These standards also enumerate the skills a student will need to be successful at the next level in their math careers at the secondary level. We met as an Algebra I course-alike group and defined the following task. We wanted each teacher to evaluate his/her own teaching structure of the Algebra classes over the past several years and label each standard and subsets with the following scale: priority skill, essential skill, and introductory skill.

Calculus

Our most talented students should be challenged with increasing expectations. A Calculus course should focus on concepts and applications. Use of a graphing calculator and other technology enables students to visualize and also to experiment with ideas and examples too tedious to calculate by hand. Students who are exposed only to contrived textbook problems with "nice" answers will never realize the true potential of mathematics in dealing with the real world.

Certainly, students will not reach this plateau without taking incremental steps to get there and develop confidence in their abilities. Over time they realize the study of mathematics requires time, patience and practice.

Goshen High School utilizes the outline provided by the Advanced Placement Program. Students are given the opportunity to take the AP exam in the spring and earn college credit for the exam. This opportunity has been made available at our school since 1985 and each year some students earn the score of 5 or 4 on the exam that earns college credit. Other students have taken the Purdue University Placement exam and earned credit there. Obviously, students must achieve at a high level to successfully continue their college study of mathematics. Previous graduates report opportunities to enroll in honors colleges or take course work at an advanced level.

Success of any program must be measured by the accomplishments of our students. We will always strive to have all our students reach their potential, understanding that sometimes, different strategies must be used for different abilities.
-JUDY DALKA

Each teacher then brought the results from each standard to the next assigned meeting and we put all of the scores on an excel spreadsheet. We then went through as a group and designed the following Algebra I Curriculum Evaluation sheets that we are currently using to guide our instruction in our classrooms. Priority ratings of our topics depict what we are expecting the students to have mastery in these areas to be successful at the next level. The essential skills level would mean that we must spend quality instructional time and have assessed students in these areas to expect students to have strong skills on these topics. The introductory level would mean that we have exposed our students to these topics but have not assessed their skill level and would not expect sufficient skill at the next level. The following is in table format of what our final findings and conclusions were on our curriculum.

Priority	Essential Skill	Introduction	Algebra One Curriculum Evaluation
			OPERATIONS WITH REAL NUMBERS
X			1.1 Compare real number expressions
X			1.2 Simplify square roots using factors
X			1.3 Understand and use the distributive, associative, and commutative properties
		X	1.4 Use the laws of exponents for rational exponents
		X	1.5 Use dimensional (unit) analysis to organize conversions and computations
			LINEAR EQUATIONS AND INEQUALITIES
X			2.1 Solve linear equations
	X		2.2 Solve equations and formulas for a specified variable
	X		2.3 Find solution sets of linear inequalities when possible numbers are given for the variable
	X		2.4 Solve linear inequalities using properties of order
		X	2.5 Solved combined linear inequalities
	X		2.6 Solve word problems that involve linear equations, formulas, and inequalities
			RELATIONS AND FUNCTIONS
		X	3.1 Sketch a reasonable graph for a given relationship
		X	3.2 Interpret a graph representing a given situation
		X	3.3 Understand the concept of a function, decide if a given relation is a function, and link equations to functions
			GRAPHING LINEAR EQUATIONS AND INEQUALITIES
X			4.1 Graph a linear equation
X			4.2 Find the slope, x-intercept, and y-intercept of a line given its graph, its equation, or two points on the line
X			4.3 Write the equation of a line in slope-intercept form. Understand how the slope and y-intercept of the graph are related
	X		4.4 Write the equation of a line given appropriate information
	X		4.5 Write the equation of a line that models a data set and use the equation (or graph of the equation) to make predictions Describe the slope of the line in terms of the data, recognizing that the slope is the rate of change.
	X		4.6 Graph a linear inequality in two variables
			PAIRS OF LINEAR EQUATIONS AND INEQUALITIES
X			5.1 Use a graph to estimate the solution of a pair of linear equations in two variables
	X		5.2 Use a graph to find the solution set of a pair of linear inequalities in two variables
X			5.3 Understand and use the substitution method to solve a pair of linear equation in two variables
X			5.4 Understand and use the addition or subtraction method to solve a pair of linear equations
X			5.5 Understand and use multiplication with the addition or subtraction method to solve a pair of linear equations in two variables
	X		5.6 Use pairs of linear equations to solve word problems
			POLYNOMIALS
X			6.1 Add and subtract polynomials
X			6.2 Multiply and divide monomials
X			6.3 Find powers and roots of monomials (only when the answer has an integer exponent)
X			6.4 Multiply polynomials
X			6.5 Divide polynomials by monomials
X			6.6 Find a common monomial factor in a polynomial
	X		6.7 Factor the difference of two squares and other quadratics
		X	6.8 Understand and describe the relationships among the solutions of an equation, the zeros of a function, the x-intercepts of a graph, and the factors of a polynomial expression

			ALGEBRAIC FRACTIONS
	X		7.1 Simplify algebraic ratios
	X		7.2 Solve algebraic proportions
			QUADRATIC, CUBIC, AND RADICAL EQUATIONS
		X	8.1 Graph quadratic, cubic, and radical equations
X			8.2 Solve quadratic equations by factoring
		X	8.3 Solve quadratic equations in which a perfect square equals a constant
		X	8.4 Complete the square to solve quadratic equations
		X	8.5 Derive the quadratic formula by completing the square
	X		8.6 Solve quadratic equations using the quadratic formula
		X	8.7 Use quadratic equations to solve word problems
		X	8.8 Solve equations that contain radical expressions
		X	8.9 Use graphing technology to find approximate
			MATHEMATICAL REASONING AND PROBLEM SOLVING
	X		9.1 Use a variety of problem-solving strategies, such as drawing a diagram, making a chart, guess-and-check, solving a simpler problem, writing an equation, and working backwards.
	X		9.2 Decide whether a solution is reasonable in the context of the original situation
	X		9.3 Use the properties of the real number system and the order of operations to justify the steps of simplifying functions and solving equations
	X		9.4 Understand that the logic of equation solving begins with the assumption that the variable is a number that satisfies the equation and that the steps taken when solving equations create new equations that have, in most cases, the same solution set as the original. Understand that similar logic applies to solving systems of equations simultaneously.
	X		9.5 Decide whether a given algebraic statement is true always, sometimes, or never (statements involving linear or quadratic expressions, equations, or inequalities
	X		9.6 Distinguish between inductive and deductive reasoning identifying and providing examples of each.
	X		9.7 Identify the hypothesis and conclusion in a logical deduction
	X		9.8 Use counterexamples to show that statements are false, recognizing that a single counterexample is sufficient to prove a general statement false.

In this technological age, mathematics is more important than ever. When students leave school, they are more and more likely to use mathematics in their work and everyday lives – operating computer equipment, planning timelines and schedules, reading and interpreting data, comparing prices, managing personal finances, and completing other problem-solving tasks. What they learn in mathematics and how they learn it will provide an excellent preparation for a challenging and ever-changing future.

Understanding the breadth of what our students are expected to master is critical. These standards can be overwhelming, particularly in light of the limited amount of time that may be available for students. This is why we use before and after school programs and double blocked classes, along with SRT. Freshmen Algebra I students are required to do remediation work outside of class. The state of Indiana has established the following mathematics standards to make clear to teachers, students, and parents what knowledge, understanding, and skills students should acquire in Algebra I:

Standard 1 – Operations With Real Numbers
Students deepen their understanding of real numbers by comparing expressions involving square roots and exponents. They use the properties of real numbers to simplify algebraic formulas, and they convert between different measurement units using dimensional analysis.

Standard 2 – Linear Equations and Inequalities
Students solve linear equations to find the value of the variable and they rearrange formulas. They solve linear inequalities by using order properties of the real numbers, and they solve word problems involving linear equations, inequalities, and formulas.

Standard 3 – Relations and Functions
Students draw and interpret graphs of relations. They understand the concept of a function, find domains and ranges, and link equations to functions.

Standard 4 – Graphing Linear Equations and Inequalities
Students draw graphs of straight lines and relate their equations to their slopes and intercepts. They model situations with linear equations and use them to make predictions, and they graph linear inequalities in two variables.

Standard 5 – Pairs of Linear Equations and Inequalities
Students solve pairs of linear equations in two variables using both graphs and algebraic methods. They use pairs of linear equations to solve word problems, and they use graphs to solve pairs of linear inequalities in two variables.

Standard 6 – Polynomials
Students operate with polynomials, adding, subtracting, multiplying, dividing, and raising to powers. They find factors of polynomials, learning special techniques for factoring quadratics. They understand the relationships among the solutions of an equation, the zeros of a function, the x-intercepts of a graph, and the factors of a polynomial.

Standard 7 – Algebraic Fractions
Students simplify algebraic fractions, using what they have learned about factoring polynomials. They solve algebraic proportions.

Standard 8 – Quadratic, Cubic, and Radical Equations
Students draw graphs of quadratic, cubic, and rational functions. They derive the formula for solving quadratic equations and solve these equations by using the formula, by factoring, and by completing the square. They also solve equations that contain radical expressions and use graphing calculators to find approximate solutions of equations.

Standard 9 – Mathematical Reasoning and Problem Solving
In a general sense, mathematics is problem solving. In all of their mathematics, students use problem-solving skills: they choose how to approach a problem, they explain their reasoning, and they check their results. At this level, students apply these skills to justifying the steps in

simplifying functions and solving equations and to deciding whether algebraic statements are true. They also learn about inductive and deductive reasoning and how to use counterexamples to show that a general statement is false.

If our view is narrowed to passing the graduation exam, it would be easy to overlook the continuing needs and expectations as they move up the math ladder of classes. As part of their instruction and assessment, students should also develop the following learning skills by Grade 12 that are woven throughout the mathematics standards:

Communication
The ability to read, write, listen, ask questions, think, and communicate about math will develop and deepen students' understanding of mathematical concepts. Students should read text, data, tables, and graphs with comprehension and understanding. Their writing should be detailed and coherent, and they should use correct mathematical vocabulary. Students should write to explain answers, justify mathematical reasoning, and describe problem-solving strategies.

Representation
The language of mathematics is expressed in words, symbols, formulas, equations, graphs, and data displays. The concept of one-fourth may be described as a quarter, 1/4, one divided by four, 0.25, 1/8 + 1/8, 25 percent, or an appropriately shaded portion of a pie graph. Higher-level mathematics involves the use of more powerful representations: exponents, logarithms, π, unknowns, statistical representation, and algebraic and geometric expressions. Mathematical operations are expressed as representations: +, =, divide, square. Representations are dynamic tools for solving problems and communicating and expressing mathematical ideas and concepts.

Connections
Connecting mathematical concepts includes linking new ideas to related ideas learned previously, helping students to see mathematics as a unified body of knowledge whose concepts build upon each other. Major emphasis should be given to ideas and concepts across mathematical content areas that help students see that mathematics is a web of closely connected ideas (algebra, geometry, the entire number system). Mathematics is also the common language of many other disciplines (science, technology, finance, social science, geography) and students should learn mathematical concepts used in those disciplines. Finally, students should connect their mathematical learning to appropriate real-world contexts.

Our final phase two challenge has been the organization of course-alike assessments. We have developed within a course (for example Algebra I) what we call form tests. These are 10-15 question assessment tests given to all students taking Algebra One; we usually give these assessments two/three weeks after a unit. These are strictly graded as either correct or wrong (no partial credit is given). These tests are designed and reviewed by group members within that course alike.

The data is then collected and we are in the growing pain stages of really using the data to benefit student learning and driving changes within our instructional strategies per classroom. One of the current difficulties that we are having is in the time needed to turn around data in a useful and timely manner.

Each year approximately 100 GHS students attend the neighboring career center. In addition, the school building/trades class has built 27 houses over the years. The school's CAD program provides entry-level designers to local businesses, many of whom begin in the spring prior to graduation.

The structure that we are currently using with our form tests is that it counts as a 30-point test in the individual teachers' classroom. Each student has up to five tries per form test and we take the average of the two best form tests as their 30-point percentage. The first two or three chances are given as whole class assessments and then students have the remaining two or three tries to sign up on their own to come in to take the current form. We have five different forms of the same type of questions to distribute to our students. Although at this point in time we are still in the growing stages of truly using course-alike meetings for significant student growth, we as a department have felt that it has been a very educational, professional development activity for us as math teachers.

The example of a form test gives feedback about concepts that students are able to retain. Often, students can learn material, but soon forget the important information. Form tests assist teachers and students in tracking retention of important concepts. The use of these assessments will become a bigger and bigger part of our planning in the future because this information points directly at our instruction. We look forward to those conversations and working within our department to provide the changes necessary for our students.

Form Test #3
Form C

Name:_____   Period:_____

1) $-5 = 3y - 4$ 1)_____	2) $-28 = 7x$ 2)_____
3) $-.03x = .09$ 3)_____	4) $-32 = -5(x + 2) + 3$ 4)_____
5) $\dfrac{2x-1}{3} = -5$ 5)_____	6) $51x - 56 = 44x$ 6)_____
7) $5x + 2(1 - x) = 2(2x - 1)$ 7)_____	8) Solve for r: $D = r*t$ 8)_____
9) $7(x + 1) - 4(5 - 2x) = -5(x - 9)$ 9)_____	10) $\dfrac{2x-5}{5} = \dfrac{x-4}{2}$ 10)_____

There is also a sense that this has helped open up communication lines within our department. It has definitely developed a sharing of the load commitment among teachers in the same course. It has also helped us to focus on the essential skills and areas that need to be stressed according to our curriculum evaluation that were previously mentioned.

The final phase of the triathlon is to close the achievement gap. We currently have in place in the English and Math content areas Individual Remediation Plans (IRP) for each student who fails to pass the GQE state test given to all sophomores in the state of Indiana. This plan is designed by combining data from our NWEA district testing and from previous student ISTEP scores. We then set up a remediation plan using Plato software and allowing students the flexibility of using study-hall time and our after-school hours programs to work on their individualized plan for studying and improving weak skill areas. We are continuing to study data and hope to keep improving the IRP so that it will truly help each and all students perform to the best of their abilities on standardized testing and hopefully to close the gap on some of our lower skilled students with their classmates.

"The president's 2006 request includes a comprehensive proposal that builds on stronger accountability provisions at the secondary level. Schools would have greater flexibility in which interventions can take place. Of 5 recommendations, the following 2 are chosen as support for the direction of our IRP program. (2) research based dropout prevention programs; (3) technology based assessment systems to provide teachers and other school officials with regular and frequent feedback on the achievement of individual students."

The following data is a useful tool that we use to keep teachers and students and parents aware of a student's chances of passing the GQE on the first try at the 10th grade level, and we use this data to help set-up our IRP plans.

Here are some interesting facts from recent test data on ISTEP and MAP tests.

- Of 192 students that took the 8th grade ISTEP and then the GQE, 180 that passed in grade 8 passed in grade 10. Only 12 that passed in grade 8 did not pass in grade 10.
- There is an 84% correlation between grade 8 and 10 scores
- 486 is the cut for both grade 8 and 10
  - Students that scored 496 or higher had a 95% passing rate in Grade 10 with 3% no score and 2% failing
  - Students that were between 496 and 476 in grade 8 passed at a 71% rate
  - Students below 476 in grade 8 passed at a 36% rate
  - Students below 440 in grade 8 passed at a 10% rate
- There is also a high correlation of 86% between 9th grade MAP and GQE scores
  - 9th graders above 240 on MAP in Spring all passed GQE
  - 9th graders between 230 and 240 on MAP had 68% passing
  - 9th graders between 220 and 230 on MAP had 17% passing
  - 9th graders below 220 only had 3% passing
- The correlation of Grade 8 Spring MAP to GQE is .86
  - Those scoring above 235 grade 8 had a 1.5% failure rate and 8.5% NS (no score) (200 students)
  - Those between 235 and 230 had a 22% failure rate and 10% NS (54 students)
  - Those between 230 and 225 had a 50% failure rate and 20% NS (41 students)

- o   **Those between 225 and 220 had a 55% failure rate and 16% NS (31 students)**
- o   **Those below 220 had a 83% failure rate (69 students)**

According to NWEA, 230 is pre-algebra level, 235 Algebra and 245 Geometry for both grades 8 and 9. The typical spring median score for grade 8 is 235, the mean 234 and for grade 9 median 244, mean 240.9. Our grade 8 is median 235, mean 235.9 and grade 9 median is 238 and mean is 239.

We continue to make efforts to collect new data and use current data for decision making both in student intervention and in teaching strategies.

Chapter 16

This is an amazing and challenging journey. The face of education is changing with teachers working together on all levels. Recently we had some teachers visit another school corporation to do a climate audit. The teachers at that school listed one of the assets for their school as being allowed to close their doors and do what they wanted. Our staff members completing this audit were taken aback at that concept. We have changed our culture from individual to collaborative because of the challenges we face together, not separately, with our students. There are still schools out there plugging along, not feeling any pressure to improve student academic performance because the community, the students and the staff are satisfied. That would not be the case with us. While to a person, our staff would point out the progress we are making, none would say that it is good enough yet. We also know that as we continue down our path, we will continue to find ways for students to do better.

The Continuing Saga

JIM KIRKTON, PRINCIPAL

In putting the finishing touches on this book, it becomes painfully obvious that a book cannot keep up with the work. We had Dennis Boswell who works for the Schlechty Center define change as nothing more than people working together. Because our people work together on a constant basis, change for us is constant—the norm.

Exactly one year ago in a meeting of our department chairs, we made a promise to write a book. Soon this will be going to the publisher and the promise will be fulfilled. It has been an excellent exercise in capturing the efforts of our fine teaching and administrative staff. Almost to the person, each contributor commented that writing this proved more difficult than first thought because as soon as the outline was completed, the sub-topics were upgraded or changed. This is the reward of working together. Nothing ever stays the same. Two months from now there will be more to add, or there is just no way to capture it all in one chapter or in one book.

Administration—Reflection/Comparison

I have taught at an elementary school in Florida, a middle school in Oregon, two large high schools, and a medium sized one school in Indiana. In those schools, teachers worked together, but usually only at a department or grade level.

The difference at Goshen High School is the widespread culture of collaboration. The leaders in the school are not condescending; they admit, "We don't have all the answers."

"We're learning together."

"We just had to try something different because business as usual was not working." The overriding question in *everything* we do is: What is best for the kids?

The learning model encompasses every aspect of the school culture. Course Alike, Student Resource Time, and other educational interventions are supported by administration. At Goshen's district level this learning culture is supported as well. Twice a month, small groups of administrators get together for book studies to discuss and support the implementation of the learning model, engagement and reflection at the building level.
-MARCEIL ROYER

At this place in time, we are focusing on improving the structures of our professional learning communities so that we can work together more efficiently. Each group has a checklist to track the various discussions the course alike groups have during their regular meetings (see Appendix). These forms are then turned in to a central source so that departmental focus can be tracked over a period of time. We think this information will be helpful as we strive to move ahead with steps two and three of the learning model.

The other focus is on finding systems and establishing protocols for making the best use of the SRT time we have thus building the school of one concept to not allow students to fall through the cracks. The focus on these areas will last far into the future.

We continue to find that teachers working with other teachers following a common vision produces a desirable result. Already this fall, teachers from area schools have gathered together to share insights and strategies for teaching English, mathematics, and social studies. Little attention has ever been paid to getting schools to work together. Because of this lack of organizational structure, schools must needlessly duplicate efforts to improve academic performance. We make the same mistakes over and over again because we do not know what the mistakes are. We miss out on the great ideas over and over because we have no forum to share this information.

Critics of education want money to be closer to the classroom, but staff development is really where the focus should lie. Not only that, but the staff development should come from professional collaboration on all levels from the classroom level, to the school level, to the state or national level. American education needs a constant and ongoing forum.

This forum is the purpose of this book. It is not our own forum that this champions, but rather it is the forum that still is to come. Educators have to gather together to solve problems. Educators have to get together with others facing similar challenges to share ideas and establish plans for action. What is not needed is a prescriptive formula designed for all when no formula can fit every situation. These formulas become another piece of paperwork that effect no change.

Because of accountability standards, most school goals have followed the English and mathematics fields for measurement. The weaknesses of this narrow thinking imposed by the political system is that the performance accountability measures used to assess progress only actually assess 3% of what schools teach. This is far too narrow of a measure and is not acceptable to all of the teachers who assist students in the subject areas of our curriculum. What is needed for schools to continue to make advancements is some type of measure for all aspects and all areas of a school program.

Why do states sponsoring high stakes testing begin to see a drop in over-all learning? This is what frightens us as this high accountability movement is based on a narrow testing field. Those outside of education simplify what we do to a level that they can understand which is limited. Those of us in education know that there is no fair way to quantify all that a school does based on one language arts and one math score given in the second year of a four year program. There is too much else including transitioning students to life after high school that is no small challenge particularly with higher percentages of second language and poverty students. To make judgments on how we are doing as a school, we must measure more than the simple scores tested on standardized tests. Schools breaking down the traditional factory structure to a more personalized environment that follows the progress of each student provide a better chance for students to succeed. That is why we call it a School of One.

As educators, not only do we need to measure all areas of the school, but also this measurement must provide information that is helpful in improving instruction. State and national accountability measures are designed instruments to impose possible penalties and do not provide information needed on a timely, instructional basis. Measurement should occur for instructional assistance and not for sanctions.

This is why we keep coming back to the learning model. This seemingly simple model provides the framework for instruction that will facilitate academic improvement through improving school structures and classroom strategies. The fluidity provided through professional learning communities working together will make positive change a constant for the generations to come. There will be no formula, no process to radically change how education happens, but rather there will be continued assessment and resulting actions to fuel the growth with the student at the center of all we do.

Our writing this book has helped us organize and capture some of what we are doing. Our hope is that it will bring about discussions among educators in the future. Our joy has been in capturing our progress at one point in time and sharing our passion for student learning.

Appendix

Example A
Checklist for Professional Learning Community reports.

Course Alike Summary Sheet
Goshen High School

Course-Alike Subject Area _____ Date_____

Members: _____   _____
               _____   _____
               _____   _____

Meeting Norms:
- Begin and end on time
- Bring materials (pacing calendar, plan book, texts, assessments, etc.)
- Stay focused on meeting topics
- Documentation of meeting content
- Other:

Course Level Planning - (horizontal)
_____ Collaborative unit planning (standards, scope, sequence of instruction)
_____ Collaborative planning for class activities
_____ Collaborative creation of student assessments—Formative
_____ Collaborative creation of student assessments-- Summative
_____ Correlation of lesson pacing
_____ Incorporation of writing in upcoming planning
_____ Revision of assignments(s) or assessments
_____ Reflection of a recent lesson/activity or instructional strategy
_____ Reflection on recent assessment
_____ Shared planning of technology implementation
_____ Data-driven instructional adjustment
_____ Discussion/planning of corrective instruction
_____ Incorporation of reading strategies
_____ Incorporation of differentiated instruction strategies
_____ Other:_____

Vertical Articulation
_____ Comparing/contrasting curricular overlap from level to the next
_____ Identification of essential skills students must master by grade level and/or by a certain
      time frame according to our established curriculum
_____ Reviewing/adjusting to address grade appropriate skills and knowledge
_____ Weeding the garden/deleting non-essential material from course instruction
_____ Discussion standards as they correlate to other levels being taught
_____ Other:_____

Tentative agenda items and goals for next Course-alike Meeting:

Example B
Our schedule is a seven period schedule, but with SRT really functions like an 8 period schedule. All teachers have assignments for six classes including the SRT period on Tuesdays and Thursdays.

Regular Schedule

Monday		Tues/Thurs		Wed/Fri	
Period 1 8:20 - 9:08		Period 2 8:20 – 9:50		Period 1 8:20 – 9:50	
Period 2 9:15 –10:03					
Period 3 10:10 - 11:03		Student Resource Time 9:57 – 11:27		Period 3 9:57 – 11:27	
Period 4 A	Lunch 11:01 – 11:36				
	Class 11:42 - 12:30				
Period 4 B	Class 11:08 - 11:36 Lunch 11:36 - 12:08 Class 12:10 - 12:30	Period 4 A	Lunch 11:34 - 12:04 Class 12:08 - 1:38	Period 5 A	Lunch 11:34 – 12:04 Class 12:08 - 1:38
Period 4 C	Class 11:08 - 11:50 Lunch 12:00 – 12:30	Period 4 B	Class 11:34 - 12:04 Lunch 12:04 - 12:34 Class 12:38 – 1:38	Period 5 B	Class 11:34 - 12:04 Lunch 12:04 - 12:34 Class 12:38 - 1:38
Period 5 12:37 - 1:25		Period 4 C	Class 11:34 – 12:34 Lunch 12:34 – 1:04 Class 1:08 – 1:38	Period 5 C	Class 11:34 – 12:34 Lunch 12:34 – 1:04 Class 1:08 – 1:38
Period 6 1:32 - 2:20		Period 6 1:45 – 3:15		Period 7 1:45– 3:15	
Period 7 2:27 - 3:15					

Example C

Over the summer, about 1/4 of our staff volunteered a day of their time to do strategic planning for the coming year. Included here is the agenda we followed to arrive at our conclusions. Following are the actions steps.

Goshen High School
June 10, 2005

Strategic Planning
1. To insure that all students graduate with the knowledge and skills necessary to make successful transitions to college and careers.

2. To improve academic rigor and student achievement.

3. To enhance the school climate.

4. To create personalized environments for learning and teaching.

What is essential?

How do we assess this?
    What do we know?
    What do we need to know?

Based on this information, what should we do?

The day provided us with valuable staff input into the coming school year.

Goal 1: To insure that all students graduate with the knowledge and skills necessary to make successful transitions to college and careers.

Essentials:
- Goal-setting for all students
- Making connections between learning and future plans
- Good language skills
- Broad content-area knowledge (K-12)
- Apply skills to real-life applications
- Communication between staff on specific students and on broader goals
- Develop a common set of "life skills" that can be taught and followed by all staff members
- In departments, decide what is "essential"

Assessments:

What we know:

- We know what successful students do that unsuccessful students don't do. (School Smarts)
- Many students respond to deadlines, SRT opportunities, etc.
- Students must find meaning in the learning.
- Students must have choice.
- Eli Lilly follow up on our freshmen indicates that our students are doing well in Indiana colleges.

What we need:

- Follow up assessment of our graduates. How successful are they in college and careers?
- We don't have any information after year one out of GHS.
- Assessments to see if students are setting goals and working toward them.
- Indicators for post-graduate success (Credentialing: A Readiness Rubric?)

Next Steps (Prioritize):

- Develop the skills needed for students to be successful in school. These are skills that are not content-area specific.
- Students need the opportunity to set short and long term goals.
- Create and implement an effective credentialing process, one that is both descriptive and prescriptive.
- Students must be able to connect what they are learning to their future plans.
- The SRT Committee should pull together some of these items and phase them into practice in the coming year(s). We need to clarify the vision of what SRT is and should become. (The steps: Awareness, Buy-in, Commitment)
- Continue to find ways to measure our students' success in post-GHS settings.

Goal 3: To enhance school climate.

Essentials:

- Trust enough to take a risk
- Trust enough to count on people
- Students and staff must be connected to each other and to the school; people must feel a part of what we are trying to do. We need to get students and staff involved.
- We are a big school. Students cannot feel "lost" in the school.
- Students and staff must feel like they have a say in what happens in school. Not everything can be dictated.
- We need a sense of pride by students and staff toward GHS
- This must be a safe environment.
- Our staff must be careful about what we say about student activities. Our actions must support the students.
- Civility and respect in both language and action by our staff and students are imperative.
- Positive relationships are essential: Student to student, student to staff, and staff to staff.

Assessments:

What we know:

- GHS is not always a safe place for all students.
- Students responded positively to safety efforts.
- We have discipline records (showing some improvement)
- We have results of the student engagement survey
- We have results of the guidance survey on student concerns
- Most kids that are involved do well in school.
- We are being pulled in lots of directions, and our resources are being stretched.

What we need to know:

- What sort of activities do students really want to be involved in? We can't just base our options on traditions.
- Do all people understand the vision?
- What keeps students from getting involved in school activities?

What we should do next (Prioritize):

- We need to create and implement plans that get students involved in activities. ENL students must be included and welcomed into activities.
- We should create an environment where money does not get in the way of student involvement.
- We need to look at ways to build relationships in the staff.
- Are there ways for students to work on student discipline issues?
- We have a PR obligation to inform the students, parents, and the community of the positive things that are going on at GHS. This helps the staff climate and with community relations. Our staff needs to be kept informed about what these positive things are.
- We must prioritize our efforts and focus our energies. If we have things to add, what will we drop?
- Celebrate our successes. This lets students and staff know that their efforts are appreciated.

In summary:

We should focus our efforts in the coming year on SRT in order to make it more effective in a variety of ways.

- Transition in and out of GHS
- Improve academics
- Improve school climate
- Create personalized environments

Example D

With leadership developing around the building, communication becomes a vital necessity. "In the Loop" informs staff members so we can use the same vocabulary and understand purpose.

January 4, 2005

Open Hours for the Media Center

Starting this week on Monday, using Smaller Learning Communities Grant monies, the Media Center will be open after school during the following times:
- Mondays, Wednesdays, and Thursdays from 4:00-6:00 p.m.
- Tuesdays from 4:00-8:00 p.m.
- Students who need transportation home can ride the bus, which leaves at 5:30.

Marilyn Graber and Lisa Evers will staff the library. Lisa's background is in office administration, and she was a researcher for a law firm. She can help students with the whole Microsoft Office Suite and obviously has considerable researching skills. It goes without saying that you all know about Marilyn's skills—so why did I include it anyway?

Remember DuFour's Third Question: "What do we do about it?" This program is a tremendous opportunity to get extra time and support for our students. It will, however, fail if we don't get students to attend. Some suggestions:
- Every SRT teacher should let students know that this time is available and give information about what kind of help students can get. Ask Theresa, Marilyn, Lisa, or an administrator if you need more details.
- Teachers, call parents and "assign" students to the after school program in order to make up late work or get extra help on assignments.
- Encourage students to meet in the media center after school for group projects.
- Technology is available. Do you have students without access? It's here. Get them to use it!
- Coaches, "assign" your athletes to the media center if their grades are slipping.
- Assign students to PLATO for ISTEP remediation or to the SAT Review program. Information on these possibilities will come in a later memo.

As required by the SLC grant, Theresa Collins will track attendance and results. You can email Lisa Evers (levers) if you are assigning specific work to specific students.

Now you know. You're officially in the loop. Pl

Example E

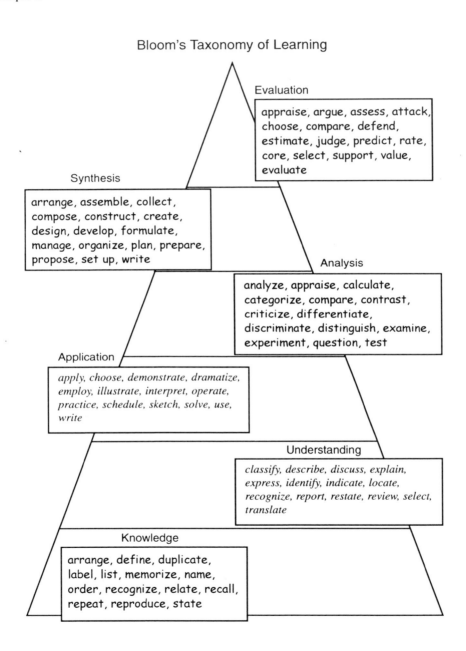

Bloom's Taxonomy of Learning

Evaluation

appraise, argue, assess, attack, choose, compare, defend, estimate, judge, predict, rate, core, select, support, value, evaluate

Synthesis

arrange, assemble, collect, compose, construct, create, design, develop, formulate, manage, organize, plan, prepare, propose, set up, write

Analysis

analyze, appraise, calculate, categorize, compare, contrast, criticize, differentiate, discriminate, distinguish, examine, experiment, question, test

Application

apply, choose, demonstrate, dramatize, employ, illustrate, interpret, operate, practice, schedule, sketch, solve, use, write

Understanding

classify, describe, discuss, explain, express, identify, indicate, locate, recognize, report, restate, review, select, translate

Knowledge

arrange, define, duplicate, label, list, memorize, name, order, recognize, relate, recall, repeat, reproduce, state

Example F

We host wider gatherings within our athletic conference and in Northern Indiana. Our purpose is to stimulate conversations among teachers to move the learning model and professional learning to a wider network. This is the registration form for a social studies local area conference.

Social Studies Super Conference

When:
Tuesday, March 8th
8:00 am – 12:00

Where:
Maple City Chapel

US 33 South – Behind Campbell & Fetter Bank

Special Guest:
Chris McGrew

Indiana Department of Education

Agenda will include

- Explanation of course-alike groups and other multi-school conferences
- Introduction of Core 40 social studies assessments
- Examination the Core 40 assessments in the areas of Economics, Government, World History and U.S. History

Social Studies
http://www.goshenschools.org/staff/swilfong/NorthernIndianaSocialStudies.htm

Coffee and light refreshments available

Please register by March 1st by emailing the following information to:
swilfong@goshenschools.org

Name
School
Subject area (pick only one): Economics, Government, World History, U.S. History
Email address

Example G

2003-2004 in the Media Center

Circulation Patterns

2003-2004 School Year: 8678 items
2002-2003 School Year: 7209 items
2001-2002 School Year: 4635 items
2000-2001 School Year: 2623 items

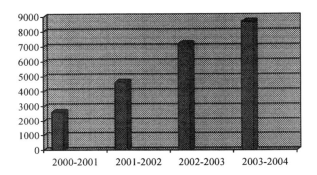

- Worked with approximately 535 classes in a variety of capacities: booktalks, teaching research strategies, assisting with research, selecting fiction, course-alike work
- Created content-area book lists for teachers who are integrating more reading
- Developed the collection further –selected new titles, ordered, cataloged and processed the new materials
- Maintained a current and accurate collection – weeded as necessary
- Conducted two staff development sessions on effective research strategies
- Compiled information literacy activities for implementation at the elementary level
- Managed the following equipment: data projectors, cassette players, digital cameras, video cameras and tripods, SMART Board, DVD player
- Completed inventory on both books and equipment
- Attended the Association of Indiana Media Educators (AIME) Conference and the Indiana Computer Educators (ICE) Conference
- Issued an average of 40 computer user names and passwords per week

Average Number of Students in the Media Center (outside of scheduled classes)

before school	10-20
lunch	10 (per lunch)
SRT	50-100
after school	25+

Example H

Check us out on the Web:

Goshen High School

http://ghs.goshenschools.org

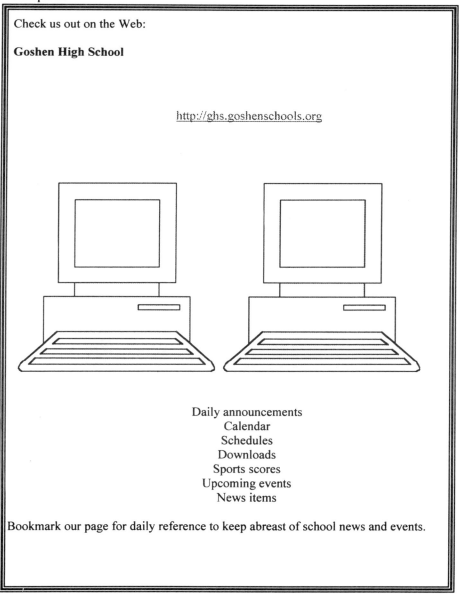

Daily announcements
Calendar
Schedules
Downloads
Sports scores
Upcoming events
News items

Bookmark our page for daily reference to keep abreast of school news and events.

About the Editors

Jim Kirkton: After 22 plus years of teaching in the English classroom, Jim made the jump to administration in winter of 1994. The biggest educational challenges came, however, after moving to Goshen in 1997 where the school was and is facing the challenges brought about by a burgeoning county population changing Goshen High School from a suburban to urban school.

The entire Kirkton family has rallied around education. Jim's wife Vicky is a career nursing educator, currently serving as dean of the Goshen College nursing department. Sons, Todd and Jonathan and daughter Sarah are math teachers (Sarah also teaches English). Their spouses Alison (elementary), Lisa (nurse) and Tim (physical education) all work in the people professions of nursing and teaching. Six grandchildren often grace the Sunday dinner table. Among father and sons and son-in-law, in addition to nearly 40 years of teaching, there are 40 years of experience coaching varsity football along with coaching other varsity sports of wrestling, track, and basketball.

Jim's classroom experiences range from teaching language arts in grades 7 through 12 in Indiana and Iowa and now couples with both middle school and high school experience in administration for the past 12 years. Extra curricular pursuits have included sponsoring school newspaper and yearbook, assisting with school musicals, and directing a school play. After years of looking for focus in staff development, one of the most interesting and rewarding staff development activities for Jim has been putting this book together with the help of the excellent Goshen High School staff.

In the best of all worlds for Jim, the Cardinals would win the World Series, the Bears would win the Superbowl, Illinois would win the Big 10, Garrison Keillor would come to town on Saturday night, and the shuffle button on the stereo would change the music after each song from country to blues to jazz to gospel to oldies to folk to local talent and end with the Mennonite national anthem, "Praise God from Whom," affectionately known as just 606. Travels would include closely following the teams and organizations of his kids (and grandkids) from school age years through college years.

Phil Lederach: Phil and his wife, Lisa, are both lifelong educators and have eight children who have come to the Lederach household from all over the world. His oldest three children are "homegrown," but the younger five are from the Marshall Islands (2), China, Taiwan, and Ohio. Between attending his children's sporting and music activities, and attending sign language classes—his youngest daughter is hard of hearing—Phil occasionally enjoys reading and writing.

Phil was a classroom English teacher for twenty-two years before becoming the assistant principal at Goshen High School. He taught middle school students in San Juan, Puerto Rico, and Hesston, Kansas, and was a high school English teacher in Middlebury, Indiana. He also coached tennis and soccer, and still enjoys playing when he gets a chance.

At times, life for Phil and his wife can be a difficult balancing act. Their work at Goshen Community Schools can become consuming and intense, and the task of raising eight children can be equally, if not more, daunting. The rewards, however, include a deep sense of satisfaction in their work, a world that is better off for their efforts, and lives that are lived fully. What more could one ask for?

About this book:

Schools today are facing increased challenges in preparing students for a workforce that requires far more skills than ever before. Gone are the unskilled, middle class jobs that previous generations held to enjoy a comfortable American lifestyle. Because we are in a world economy, those positions have been shipped overseas. Those wishing to live the middle class lifestyle must have the education and skills necessary to participate in the increasingly technological workplace. To prepare our students for this, a much higher percentage of students must have the academic preparation to continue educational pursuits beyond high school.

This book is the story of how one high school, Goshen High School, in Goshen, Indiana, is accepting this challenge. Goshen is not the only school on this journey; it is just one story. Our goal is not to create a school of students who have been drilled into submission with facts, but our goal is to create an environment where students are valued while supporting the student in individual academic pursuits. We call this a School of One and it simply means, we want a school where at least one adult knows and mentors each student in our school providing whatever intervention is necessary to assist this student in becoming successful particularly in the transition beyond high school.

The School of One has allowed us to dramatically increase academic expectation while providing the support necessary for the student to maneuver in these murky waters. This book is a story of a school constantly changing and growing to assist students. It has no answers; it is just a journey. It is not about being right; it is just about how we are facing the tremendous challenges in a community with the highest percentage of second language learners in our state coupled with increasing poverty rates. This is a story about our teachers and how they care. It is a story about our students and how they are trying.

– JIM KIRKTON, Principal

ISBN 0-9777268-0-0

90000